THE KNITTER'S BIBLE

knitte

THE KNITTER'S BIBLE
knitted BAGS

CLAIRE CROMPTON

D&C
David and Charles

A DAVID & CHARLES BOOK
Copyright © David & Charles Limited 2007

David & Charles is an F+W Publications Inc. company
4700 East Galbraith Road
Cincinnati, OH 45236

First published in the UK in 2007

Text and project designs © Claire Crompton 2007

A catalogue record for this book is available from the British Library.

ISBN-13: 978-0-7153-2326-7 paperback
ISBN-10: 0-7153-2326-1 paperback

Printed in China by SNP Leefung
for David & Charles
Brunel House   Newton Abbot   Devon

Executive Editor Cheryl Brown
Desk Editor Bethany Dymond
Head of Design Prudence Rogers
Production Controller Ros Napper
Project Editor Nicola Hodgson
Photographer Lorna Yabsley

Visit our website at www.davidandcharles.co.uk

David & Charles books are available from all good bookshops; alternatively
you can contact our Orderline on 0870 9908222 or write to us at FREEPOST EX2 110,
D&C Direct, Newton Abbot, TQ12 4ZZ (no stamp required UK only); US customers call
800-289-0963 and Canadian customers call 800-840-5220.

contents

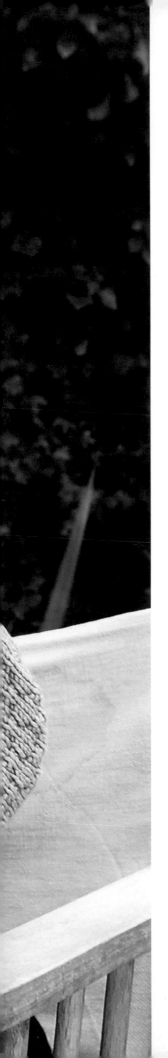

it's all in the bag!

Bags are the ultimate knitted accessory. Stylish, smart, funky or cute – you can never have too many; they are also versatile, practical and fun to knit. Whether all you need is a glamorous little item to hold your keys and your credit card, or you tend to lug half your worldly goods around with you, you'll find a project to inspire you here.

Knitted bags give you almost instant gratification. They don't take much time, they don't take much yarn, and they are a great way of experimenting with new yarns or techniques. They are always useful, and make welcome gifts for other people, too. Knit a smart bag to complete a perfect outfit, knit a roomy one to take out shopping, make a frivolous bag for fun days or a shimmering one for a night out. Make one for work, one for weekends, and one to take on holiday. Play around with fabric and texture; knit a bag in cosy tweed for the winter or in fresh, crisp cotton for hotter days.

The projects in this book begin with a simple-to-knit handbag presented in a range of different yarns to show how versatile the pattern can be. Other projects include small sophisticated bags for a smart city look, frivolous and frilly bags, bright and outrageous bags, and sturdy, adaptable and hard-wearing bags. Each project has a 'Yarn Focus' feature that explains why I chose a particular yarn for a project. There are also 'Design Secrets Unravelled' features suggesting alternative yarns and colours to give the projects a different twist; take these ideas and use them as a starting point for your own inspiration to come up with something unique.

This first section of the book focuses on the qualities and varieties of different yarns. We discuss fibres (page 9), weight (page 10), colour (page 11) and texture (page 12) and offer you advice on choosing yarns for the projects. Gauge (what knitters in the UK call tension) is an important part of knitting, and the process of measuring your gauge is clearly described on page 15. There are also hints and tips on measuring textured yarns. Written knitting instructions can

sometimes seem daunting, but the section on reading knitting patterns on pages 16–17 explains the commonly used knitting shorthand and abbreviations thoroughly.

All the techniques used for the projects in this book are explained in detail in the final section of the book (pages 100–123). There are clear diagrams and close-ups of the projects to help you all the way. I hope these will encourage you to tackle some more advanced techniques you may not have tackled before, such as cabling, intarsia, Fair Isle or making mitred squares. Bags are the perfect project for trying out new techniques, as they are small-scale and give you attractive results relatively quickly. If you require a more comprehensive guide to any knitting techniques, my previous book *The Knitter's Bible* contains everything you need to know.

When you've spent time and devotion on making something beautiful, it deserves to be finished off with the same care and attention. Pages 114–117 cover the techniques of lining bags and adding zips to give your bags a finishing touch that will make them look truly professional. We also discuss using ready-made handles and how to change the handle on a bag to create a different look.

If straightforward knitting is not quite enough to fulfil the creative artist in you, then there's a section on using simple embroidery stitches to add an extra individual touch to your bags (page 120). If you want to experiment with knitted fabrics, some of the projects in this book could be fulled; the technique for this is discussed on page 111.

Finally, it doesn't matter how accomplished a knitter you are – everyone makes mistakes sometimes. Pages 122–123 tell you how to correct any errors simply and quickly and rescue your project from disaster.

So, take your needles, find some yarn, and make something beautiful today…

in the beginning...

fibres

Knitting bags is an exciting and inexpensive way to explore the glorious range of yarns that is available today. You need only a modest amount of yarn to make a smaller bag, so you can indulge in buying some of the more luxurious yarns that might be too costly for a whole garment. Making a larger bag gives you a chance to revel in some of the more flamboyant textures or fibre mixes.

NATURAL FIBRES

Natural fibres come from either animal or plant sources. They can be more expensive than synthetic fibres, but are fantastic to knit with and will keep looking fabulous even if used for everyday bags that need to withstand a lot of wear and tear.

Alpaca is spun from the coat of the alpaca, a close relation of the llama. It is a wonderfully soft and lustrous yarn, which has many of the qualities of cashmere but at a more affordable price.

Angora yarn comes from the Angora rabbit. A yarn with a high content of angora is fluffy and tends to shed fibres. Angora is usually blended with another fibre to give it stability; it gives the yarn softness.

Cashmere is spun from the hair of the Cashmere goat. Pure cashmere yarn is very expensive; it becomes much more affordable when blended with another fibre. I have used a cashmere-and-wool mix yarn for the Off the Cuff bag (pages 32–35) for a luxurious look.

Cotton comes from the ball of the cotton plant. It is a heavy fibre and is often blended with other fibres, such as silk or wool, to lighten it. Cotton has no elasticity and items knitted with it can tend to become baggy – which is why it's a good idea to line any bag you knit with it (see pages 114–116). However, it is still a great yarn for casual summer bags. Cotton can be mercerized; this process gives it lustre and makes it take brighter dyes. Matte cotton tends to be more loosely spun and is softer. I've used some vibrant colours in matte cotton for the Fantastic Flowers bag (pages 78–81), while the Fabulous Fair Isle purses (pages 94–99) use both matte and mercerized cottons together.

Linen comes from the stem of the flax plant, and is often blended with cotton to soften it. On its own, linen drapes better than cotton. It is available in fashion colours and in traditional natural shades.

Mohair is spun from the coat of the Angora goat. The softer kid mohair is the first or second shearing of a kid goat; it is finer than the mohair from the adult goat. Mohair is usually blended with another fibre to give it strength. I wouldn't recommend it on its own for bags; it is far too hairy, would shed fibres over your clothes and would be too unstructured to hold any shape. In a yarn mix, however, it is much more stable; the Patching It Up bag (pages 28–31) uses a mohair/silk mix in bright raspberry, where it offers a superb contrast to the drier, crisper yarns. Try using mohair in your own yarn mix, to add texture and a haze of colour.

Silk is a continuous filament secreted by the silkworm larva that it spins around itself to form a cocoon. This cocoon is unwound and the fibres spun together to form a yarn. Silk is lustrous, soft, and has a dry feel. I have used silk in several of the bags, including the Hands-Free handbag (pages 54–55). It softens the whole look of the bag and gives a subtle sheen to the hot pink.

Wool is spun from the fleece of a sheep; different breeds of sheep produce different qualities of wool. Merino wool is very soft; Shetland is more hard-wearing; Wensleydale is very lustrous; and Jacob wool is spun in fantastic natural colours. I love using wool yarns, especially thick rustic tweeds, which also look great when fulled, like the Falling Leaves bag (pages 42–45). Many of the projects in this book use wool and I would always recommend it as a great yarn for the beginner to use. It knits up beautifully and can be pulled back and recycled without loss of quality.

BLENDED FIBRES

Blended yarns containing both natural and synthetic fibres combine the natural yarn's qualities with the hard-wearing stability of the synthetic. Some of the synthetic fibres used in the projects are acrylic, metallic, microfibre, nylon, polyamide fibre, polyester and viscose. Synthetic fibres are spun into fancy yarns, such as eyelash, ribbon and faux fur. The Snow Queen bag (pages 72–74) combines a long eyelash yarn and a bubbly slub yarn with smoother cotton for contrast. These yarns take dyes well and add vibrant colour to a yarn mix.

weight

Super-fine

Fine

Light

Medium

Bulky

Super-bulky

The weight of a yarn refers to its thickness; a light-weight yarn is thin, and knits up into a soft, delicate fabric. A medium-weight yarn is thicker and knits up into a chunkier fabric. Throughout this book, I encourage you to experiment with new yarns and discover how a fabric can be changed by altering the weight of yarn used. The Get Back backpack and its shoulder-bag version (pages 36–41) are both knitted to the same gauge (see page 15 for an explanation of gauge). The backpack is soft and casual knitted in a medium-weight yarn, whereas the shoulder bag is more structured and denser when knitted in a yarn mix equivalent to a bulky-weight yarn.

PLY OR THICKNESS

Yarns are sometimes described by a number of ply – for example, 2ply, 4ply or 6ply. A ply is a single twisted strand. As a general rule, the more plies that are twisted together, the thicker the yarn. However, just to confuse things, plies can be different thicknesses themselves. A tightly spun ply will be thinner than a loosely spun one. For example, a 2ply Shetland wool yarn knits up to fine-weight (4ply) gauge, whereas a thick Lopi yarn (a type of wool traditionally sourced from Iceland) is a single ply.

To avoid this confusion, I have adopted a standard developed by the Craft Yarn Council of America, which divides yarns into weight rather than number of plies. Throughout this book, I give a generic description of each yarn used, specifying the weight and type of yarn that I have used for each project. This means that you can use any yarn that is the same weight to knit your project; this is especially useful if the one featured has been discontinued, as happens frequently as yarn manufacturers update their range. (If you want to use exactly the same yarns featured in this book, see pages 124–125 for details.)

Yarn manufacturers in the US and in the UK sometimes use different names to identify the same weight of yarn. Where they differ, I have included both in the following table. Throughout this book, I give the US weight first, with the UK equivalent following in brackets.

STANDARD YARN WEIGHTS

weight	gauge*	needle size**	yarn type***
super-fine	27–32 sts	1 to 3 (2.25–3.25mm)	sock, fingering (2ply, 3ply)
fine	23–26 sts	3 to 5 (3.25–3.75mm)	sport, baby (4ply)
light	21–24 sts	5 to 7 (3.75–4.5mm)	light worsted, DK (DK)
medium	16–20 sts	7 to 9 (4.5–5.5mm)	worsted, afghan (aran)
bulky	12–15 sts	9 to 11 (5.5–8mm)	chunky
super-bulky	6–11 sts	11 (8mm) and above	super-chunky

Notes: * Gauge (tension) is measured over 4in/10cm in stockinette (stocking) stitch
       ** US needle sizes are given first, with UK equivalents in brackets
       *** Alternative US yarn type names are given first, with UK equivalents in brackets

colour

Colour is a tremendous source of inspiration for the creative knitter. Throughout this book, I have given ideas for alternative colourways for each bag along with the main colourway. Some suggest using bold and vibrant colours together for a striking look; others use a more sophisticated palette of natural earth tones. You could use several colours of a plain yarn to introduce a colour mix into your knitting, and try a technique such as intarsia or Fair Isle (see pages 108–109 and 94–99). The Fantastic Flowers bag (pages 78–81) uses a vivid and exciting clash of pink and orange, while the Classic Colours Fair Isle purse (pages 94–97) merges blues together for a softer look. You could also use multi-coloured yarns. 'Multi-coloured yarn' is a general term that I use throughout the book to describe yarns that are dyed in many colours. Within this general heading are several types of multi-coloured yarn, some of which are shown in the swatch above. These yarns are easy to use, since there is no joining in of new colours or sewing in of ends.

A GUIDE TO COLOUR
The yarns illustrated above are:

Self-striping wool yarn (1) features a long length of colour that slowly merges into the next. These lengths are usually sufficient to knit a couple of rows. I have used a yarn like this for the Get Back backpack (pages 36–39). I also used it for the Square Dance bag (pages 68–71), where each colour emerges to work a different shape and produce the patchwork effect.

Ribbon yarn (2) has shorter lengths of colour that produce splashes of colour rather than stripes. The splashes are long enough to knit several stitches but not a complete row.

Short-pile eyelash yarn (3) has short splashes of colour that are further merged through the texture of the yarn.

Long-pile eyelash yarn (4); this one has a multi-coloured strand twisted with an orange strand. The eyelash pile fluffs out from the core strands. A metallic thread is woven in to complete the impression of randomly placed colours.

Tweed yarn (5) is a marl of two or more colours with flecks of contrasting colours. Using tweed yarn introduces depth of colour to any knitted fabric. This one is a twist of ginger ply with an orange ply. The flecks are multi-coloured. I have used a tweed yarn for the Falling Leaves bag (pages 42–45) – a deep green with specks of bright orange and yellow. The Pretty in Purple lacy bag (page 49) is knitted in a wonderful dark purple tweed.

Striped yarn (6) is designed to be used for small pieces of knitting, such as socks, and some of them produce a strict stripe pattern. Others, like this one, have short stripes of colours merging into each other. You could break up the stripe sequence by using two balls and working two rows with each ball, or use two strands together to produce a marl yarn.

1 Astrakhan

2 Bouclé

3 Chenille

4 Cord

5 Eyelash

6 Matte cotton

texture

Yarns are made in a wide range of textures, from plain, plied yarns to extravagant concoctions of ribbon, bouclé or eyelash. I made these tassels to illustrate the wonderful diversity of yarn textures. Each one shows the qualities of the yarn and what type of fabric it makes when knitted. A simple stockinette stitch reveals how fabulous the textured yarns are; small patterned stitches would be lost in the texture, but how about trying a really chunky cable worked in the astrakhan or a frivolous lace stitch worked in the mohair?

A GUIDE TO TEXTURE

The yarns are described below:

1 Astrakhan yarn has a texture of loose snarls that curl across the surface of the fabric. Use a simple stockinette stitch to display its texture fully (see the Secret Life shoulder bag, pages 40–41).

2 Bouclé has a similar looped texture to astrakhan, formed when a loosely spun strand is allowed to wrap around itself into snarls and snags. This cotton bouclé is crisp and produces a dense texture somewhat like a towel. Softer bouclés in mohair and wool make a luxuriously deep fabric.

3 Chenille is a short-pile yarn; it produces a wonderfully rich velvety fabric. This chunky version would be great on its own; a thinner chenille would add softness and luxury into a yarn mix.

8 Metallic

7 Mercerized cotton

9 Mohair

10 Ribbon

11 Tape

12 Tweed

4 Cord is a smooth, round yarn. When knitted, each stitch sits apart from its neighbours, producing a more open fabric. This is great for clearly defined knit and purl fabrics, and adds structure to a softer yarn mix.

5 Eyelash yarn looks somewhat like a frayed ribbon. Available in width from very narrow to outrageously wide, it knits up into a fabric of deep shimmering waves. Contrast it with smoother yarns, or use a longer-pile version for a fluffy trim (see the Snow Queen bag, pages 72–74).

6 Matte cotton has a lovely dry texture; it has weight and will add strength and structure to a yarn mix. The colour of this cotton/silk mix is beautifully dusty, like painted plaster.

7 Mercerized cotton is a tight, lustrous yarn that makes a very clean, crisp fabric. It is available in wide range of bright, intense colours.

8 Metallic yarns are crunchy, modern and full of light. This is a mix of viscose and metallic elements that would add a sharp highlight in a soft fluid fabric. Add it to any yarn mix to create instant glamour and sparkle.

9 Mohair is a soft, fluffy yarn; its fibres trap air and light to produce a feather-soft fabric. Use in a mix with heavier yarns to add a haze of colour (see the In a Flap bag, pages 26–27).

10 Ribbon is a woven version of tape. It is flat, and varies in width from narrow to wide. These yarns are available in any fibre from wool through to modern synthetics. The ladder ribbon featured here has a strong structure punctuated with sharp stabs of precise colour. Ribbon yarns are very varied; they can be multi-coloured, stranded with metallic fibres, open or solid structures, fluffy or crisp, slinky or hard.

11 Tape is a fluid knitted flat yarn that rarely produces a completely flat fabric; it tends to twist and fold on your needles. It might fold in half for one stitch and then open out for the next. This cotton version makes a fabric with structure, but a viscose version produces a wonderfully slinky fabric.

12 Tweed yarn is a combination of two or more colours, spun together or introduced as slubs or knots of colour. A knitted tweed fabric looks warm, cosy and resilient. You can contrast it with metallic or cotton for an exciting twist. Pure wool tweed makes fantastic fulled fabric; the colours merge into a dense brushed fabric.

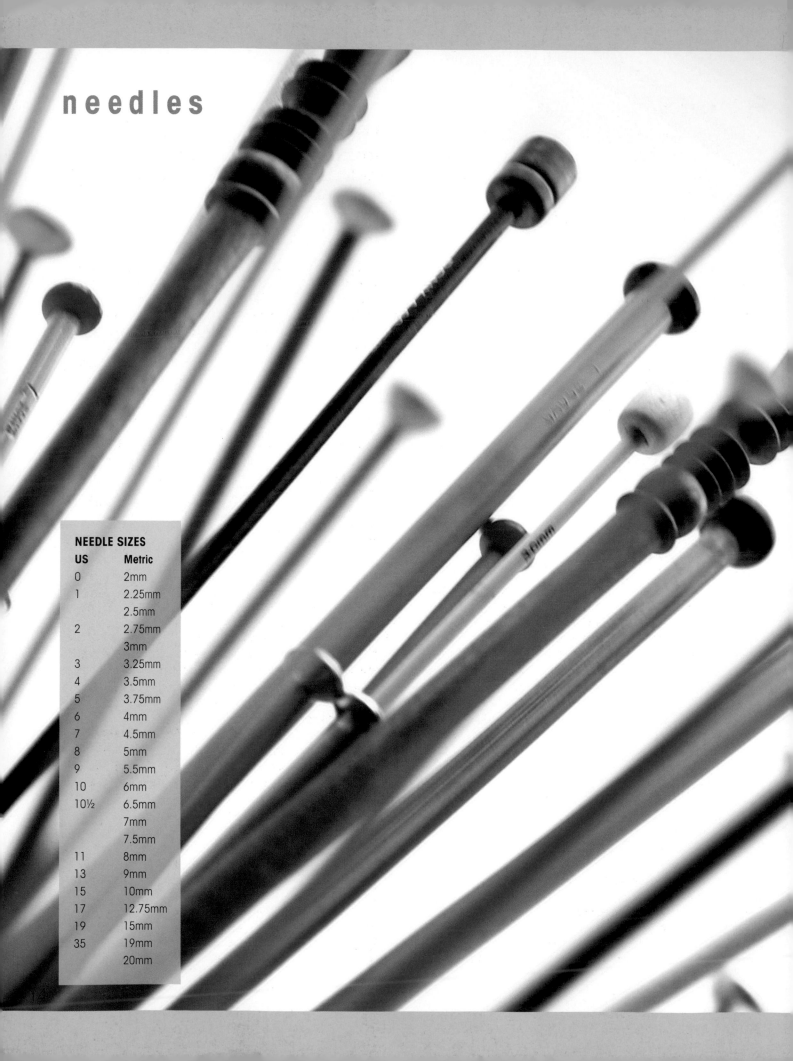

needles

NEEDLE SIZES

US	Metric
0	2mm
1	2.25mm
	2.5mm
2	2.75mm
	3mm
3	3.25mm
4	3.5mm
5	3.75mm
6	4mm
7	4.5mm
8	5mm
9	5.5mm
10	6mm
10½	6.5mm
	7mm
	7.5mm
11	8mm
13	9mm
15	10mm
17	12.75mm
19	15mm
35	19mm
	20mm

needles

gauge

At the beginning of every project, I have given the gauge (tension) that you need to achieve to make the project successfully. The gauge is the number of stitches and rows you need to make a one-inch (2.5cm) square. This is a very important part of knitting; if you do not obtain the correct gauge, the bag will not be the correct size. This is especially significant when you are knitting a bag to a specific size; for example, the When the Cows Come Home bag (pages 60–63) may finish up too small or the Quick Draw drawstring bags (pages 72–77) too big.

GAUGE MEASUREMENTS

The gauge is given over 4in (10cm). For example: the gauge for a light-weight (DK) yarn is 22 stitches and 28 rows to 4in (10cm) measured over stockinette (stocking) stitch on size 6 (4mm) needles. To check your gauge, you must work a square of fabric measuring at least 6in (15cm), using the stated yarn, needle size and stitch. You can then measure the fabric in the middle of the square, avoiding the edge stitches (as these will be distorted).

Sometimes it is difficult to achieve both the correct stitch and row count. It is more important to obtain the correct stitch count, so concentrate on achieving that. The row count matters only in projects where I have given shaping instructions over a certain number of rows, such as the Bowled Over bag (pages 56–59) and the Buttons and Bows bag (pages 82–85).

KNITTING A GAUGE SQUARE

To knit a gauge square in stockinette stitch, cast on the number of stitches stated for 4in (10cm) plus half as many again. For example: 22 sts plus 11 sts.

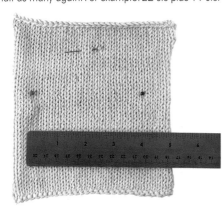

1 Work in stockinette stitch for 6in (15cm) and then bind off loosely.
2 Steam or wet press the square in the way that you will use for your finished project (see page 112). The information on the ball band will tell you whether you can steam the yarn or not.

3 Lay the square on a flat surface without stretching it. Place a ruler horizontally on the square and place a pin 1in (2.5cm) in from the edge and place another at 4in (10cm) from the first pin.
4 Do the same for the rows by placing the ruler vertically, keeping away from the cast-on and bound-off edges, which may pull the fabric in.
5 Count the number of stitches and rows between the pins: this is your gauge. If you have more stitches than the suggested number, your stitches are too small; you will need to use a size larger needle to make the stitches bigger and so obtain fewer stitches to 4in (10cm). If you have too few stitches, this means your stitches are too big; you need to use a size smaller needle to make the stitches smaller and so obtain more to 4in (10cm).
6 Work another square until you achieve the gauge stated in the pattern.

MEASURING TEXTURED YARNS

If you are using a textured yarn, it can be difficult to see individual stitches and rows. For yarns with a long pile, such as the faux fur shown, measure the 4in (10cm) for stitches and rows, placing a marker in a contrasting yarn. Leave long ends on these markers so they are visible through the long pile. Hold the square up to a window or a light (protect your eyes against a strong light). This will show up the stitches and rows clearly for you to count.

With yarns that are heavily textured, such as the bouclé shown, or a thick fleece or plush yarn, the stitches close up and make a uniform surface when knitted. Knit a contrasting coloured sewing cotton in with the yarn. This will show up the stitches and rows and make counting easier. Mark the 4in (10cm) for stitches and rows with a contrasting thread, so you can pull the fabric to make out difficult stitches without losing any pins.

It is often easier to make out the stitches and rows on the wrong side of the square, on the reverse stockinette side, so use this side to measure over.

If you are not sure what the individual stitches and rows look like, refer to page 103.

MEASURING OVER A STITCH PATTERN

If the gauge is given for a stitch pattern like that for the Buttons and Bows bag (pages 82–85), cast on enough stitches to work complete repeats. The repeat of the pattern follows the asterisk; cast on a multiple of this number of stitches plus any stitches given at the beginning and the end of the row.

USING GAUGE FOR SUBSTITUTING YARNS

For all these projects, I have suggested other yarns to use or different weights of yarn to mix up into a unique yarn. It is very important to keep aiming for the stated gauge when you alter the yarn mix, or the project will not be the correct size and the finished fabric may be too loose or too tight.

abbreviations

Abbreviations are used in knitting patterns to shorten commonly used terms so that the instructions are easier to read and a manageable length. The following is a list of all the abbreviations you need to make the projects in this book.

alt	alternate
approx	approximately
beg	begin/beginning
cm	centimetre(s)
cont	continue
dec(s)	decrease(s)/decreasing
DK	double knitting
foll	following
g	gram
g st	garter stitch (k every row)
in(s)	inch(es)
inc(s)	increase(s)/increasing
k	knit
k2tog	knit 2 stitches together (decrease 1 stitch)
k3tog	knit 3 stitches together (decrease 2 stitches)
LH	left hand
m	metre(s)
mm	millimetre(s)
M1	make one (increase 1 stitch)
MB	make a bobble
oz	ounces
p	purl
patt(s)	pattern(s)
patt rep(s)	pattern repeat(s)
p2tog	purl 2 stitches together (decrease 1 stitch)
p3tog	purl 3 stitches together (decrease 2 stitches)
psso	pass slipped stitch over
rem	remain/ing

rep(s)	repeat(s)
rev st st	reverse stockinette stitch (1 row p, 1 row k)
RH	right hand
RS	right side
sk2po	slip 1 stitch, knit 2 stitches together, pass slipped stitch over (decrease 2 stitches)
ssk	slip 2 stitches one at a time, knit 2 slipped stitches together (decrease 1 stitch)
ssp	slip 2 stitches one at a time, purl 2 slipped stitches together through the back of the loops (decrease 1 stitch)
sl	slip
st(s)	stitch(es)
st st	stockinette stitch (1 row k, 1 row p) (UK: stocking stitch)
tog	together
WS	wrong side
wyib	with yarn in back
wyif	with yarn in front
yd(s)	yard(s)
yfwd	yarn forward
yo	yarn over
*	repeat directions following * as many times as indicated or until end of row
( )	repeat instructions in round brackets the number of times

In the instructions for the projects, I have favoured US knitting terms. Refer to this box for the UK equivalent.

US TERM	UK TERM
bind off	cast off
gauge	tension
stockinette stitch	stocking stitch
reverse stockinette stitch	reverse stocking stitch
seed stitch	moss stitch
moss stitch	double moss stitch

reading knitting patterns

A knitting pattern tells you how to knit and make up a knitted project. The instructions use shorthand phrases and abbreviations, otherwise they would be far too long. The abbreviations used in this book appear in a list on page 16 with an explanation of what they mean. Many are commonly used, such as k and p. Others refer to special stitches, like C4F. These are explained in the pattern and in the technique section at the back (see page 110 for cables).

SPECIAL INSTRUCTIONS

In one of the projects, the Instant Messenger bag (pages 86–89), I have put instructions for the cable panels outside the main project instructions. This is because these panels would make the project instructions very long and complicated, and a lot of information would be repeated. The panel is set within a group of stitches; keep following the pattern panel while working your way through the project instructions. For example: **Row 1** (K1, p1) twice, C4F, p2, work row 1 of panel A, p2, C4B, p2, work row 1 of panel B, p2, C4F, p2, work row 1 of panel C, p2, C4B, (p1, k1) twice.

WORKING FROM CHARTS

The Fantastic Flowers bag (pages 78–81), the When the Cows Come Home bag (pages 60–63) and the Fabulous Fair Isle purses (pages 94–99) are all worked from colour charts. There are usually very little written instructions for these, apart from how many stitches to cast on and knitting that is not included on the chart. Working from charts is explained, along with the technique for intarsia, on pages 108–109.

Sometimes the chart shows any shaping that has to be done, and this will be included in the instructions to set the chart. For example: Working RS rows (odd) from right to left and WS rows (even) from left to right, and dec 1 st at each end of 13th and every foll 8th row, work in st st from chart until the 64th row has been completed. 52 sts.

COMMON SHORTHAND PHRASES

You will see some common shorthand phrases appearing in the pattern instructions. These include the following:

Cont as set Instead of repeating the same instructions over and over, the pattern tells you to continue working as previously told. For example: Cont in cable patt as set, commencing with row 5 of panels, until flap measures approx 11in (28cm) from beg.

Keeping patt correct Continue with a stitch pattern, keeping it correctly worked over the correct number of stitches, while doing something that may interfere with the stitch pattern. For example: Keeping texture patt correct, dec 1 st (as set on row 40) at each end of every foll 6th row to 55 sts.

Work as given for This is used to avoid repeating instructions; it can be used within one set of instructions or to show how to work another version of the same bag. For example: Work as given for Summertime Sweetie bag, omitting the drawstring strap.

* repeat directions following * as many times as indicated or until end of row. For example: **Row 1** K1, *p1, k1; rep from * to end.

** usually appears at the beginning or at the beginning and the end of a section of instructions and indicates that several rows of instructions should be repeated. For example: Work as given for first strap from ** to **.

( ) you should repeat instructions in round brackets the number of times indicated. For example: K1, (ssk, k5) 7 times, ssk, k6.

IMPERIAL AND METRIC MEASUREMENTS

Noted that the patterns are written in both imperial (inches and ounces) and metric (centimetres and grams) measurements. You should stick to one or the other; some imperial to metric measurements are not exact conversions.

Throughout this book, any special instructions that are required to complete a project, such as the details for the cable panel on this Instant Messenger bag, are provided separately from the main project instructions.

and now
to knit...

simply chic bags

Here are five versions of one simple bag pattern that proves that knowing the basics of how to cast on, knit and purl, and bind off are all you need to create a beautiful bag. We start off with a funky fake-fur version. Two of the other bags are knitted in light-weight (DK) yarns; the purple and wedding versions rely on a mixture of textures for their impact. Medium-weight (aran) yarn is used for the rose version. The chunky version shows how to convert any of these variations into a shoulder bag. I've offered different ideas for trimmings, handles and fastenings, so it is easy to alter the basic pattern to create your own ideal bag.

Fake-fur yarns are a great way to use minimum effort for maximum impact. This pattern is very simple, even for less experienced knitters, but the lush eyelash yarn creates a wonderful fabric. See pages 21–22.

This glamorous version demonstrates how you can exploit colour, texture and trimmings to create interest. The pattern is still very simple, but it's the imaginative use of contrasting yarns and stylish embellishments that gives this bag its beauty. See page 23.

Working a bag in strips of several yarns in the same colourway creates a bag full of subtle texture and interest. This version also features some pretty trimmings; always keep a look out for special ribbons and beads that you can incorporate into your knitted pieces. See page 24.

You can use a simple bag as the background to some stunning knitted leaves and roses. This wonderful little bag offers an eye-catching colour contrast in three dimensions. See page 25.

This version of the simply chic bag adds a useful shoulder strap and a flap secured by a contrasting diamanté brooch. This choice of yarn creates a lovely fabric that is cosily chunky, soft and yet resilient. See pages 26–27.

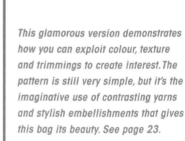

just fur you

MEASUREMENTS
Finished bag measures 8in (20.5cm) wide and 9in (23cm) high

GATHER TOGETHER...
Materials
2 x 1¾oz (50g) balls of bulky-weight (chunky) eyelash yarn (44yd/40m per ball) in brown/black
Oddment of black light-weight (DK) yarn for sewing up and attaching handles

Needles and notions
1 pair of size 10½ (7mm) needles
Pair of black plastic handles 6in (15cm) wide at base
Lining fabric 20in (51cm) x 12in (30.5cm)

GAUGE
12½ sts and 17 rows to 4in (10cm) measured over st st using size 10½ (7mm) needles

YARN FOCUS
I love the simplicity of working with eyelash yarn. The fuzziness hides any shaping or complicated stitches, making them unnecessary. The yarn produces a thick and luxurious fabric, which is just what I wanted for this bag.

The beauty of this bag lies in its fabulous fake-fur effect. The bag itself is very simple in its construction: just knit two pieces of fabric and sew them together. Cast on, knit in stockinette stitch, bind off, and you are done. Sew on some bought handles as a classy finishing touch.

Knit your bag...
Front and back (work 2 the same)
Using size 10½ (7mm) needles, cast on 24 sts.
Work in st st (1 row k, 1 row p), starting with a k row, until front measures 8½in (21.5cm) from beg, ending with a k row.
Knit 3 rows.
Bind off purlwise.

to finish...
Make a simple lining as shown on pages 114–115. Using light-weight (DK) yarn, join the side and base seams. Sew the handles in position, making sure they are central, by working several stitches through holes in the handle and then through the top edge of the bag. With WS together, slip the lining into the bag and slipstitch into place below the bound-off edge.

Eyelash yarns with a long pile produce a wonderful texture for knitted bags.

DESIGN SECRETS UNRAVELLED...
Fashion yarns such as long eyelash yarns and fake fur are best worked in simple shapes in stockinette stitch. Bags are usually a simple shape anyway, and these yarns give them high impact without much effort. This bag doesn't take much yarn, so you can spend a little more and buy a wildly extravagant yarn or one that you wouldn't dare use for a sweater.

MEASUREMENTS
Finished bag measures 8in (20.5cm) wide
and 9in (23cm) high

GATHER TOGETHER...
Materials
A 1 x 1¾oz (50g) ball of light-weight (DK) silky-
look yarn (147yd/135m per ball) in light purple
B 1 x 1¾oz (50g) ball of light-weight (DK) tape
(127yd/116m per ball) in dark purple

Needles and notions
1 pair of size 6 (4mm) needles
9in (23cm) of bead trim
Button
Lining fabric 20in (51cm) x 12in (30.5cm)

GAUGE
22 sts and 28 rows to 4in (10cm) measured over
st st using size 6 (4mm) needles and yarn A

YARN FOCUS
For this bag, I chose a soft silky-look yarn with a
subtle texture, contrasted with a denser tape with
a suede feel. It turned out that the tape yarn was
very stretchy and so pulled in the top of the bag.
The bead fringe, bought ready-attached to a ribbon,
was a simple way to add sparkle, while the button
added a further accent of interest and colour.

Here, two luxurious yarns in shades of purple with the addition of some
glamorous bead trim create a gorgeous evening bag. Simple stockinette stitch
is used with a narrow garter stitch edging at the top. The stockinette stitch
handles are left to roll to create a soft tube. This is a basic square bag that has
been shaped without any decreasing of stitches because of the yarn choice.

Knit your bag...
Front and back (work 2 the same)
Using size 6 (4mm) needles and A, cast on 44 sts.
Work in st st (1 row k, 1 row p), starting with a k
row, until front measures 6in (15cm) from beg,
ending with a p row.
Change to B and cont in st st until front measures
8½in (21.5cm) from beg, ending with a k row.
Knit 3 rows.
Bind off purlwise.

Handles (make 2)
Using size 6 (4mm) needles and B, cast on 66 sts.
Work 6 rows in st st.
Bind off.

to finish...
Press back and front according to instructions on
ball bands. Do not press the handles; leave them to
roll. Make a simple lining as shown on pages 114–
115. Join the side and base seams of the bag.
Sew on the bead trim on the front only. Sew on the
handles, making sure they are central, with the rev
st st side facing out. Sew the button onto the front,
making sure it is central. Make a button loop from
yarn B: thread one strand of the yard onto a sewing
needle, and tie a knot in one end. Thread through
the back of the bag at the top from the WS to RS,
around the button and return to the back, threading
through from RS to WS. Secure end. With WS
together, slip the lining into the bag and slipstitch
into place below the bound-off edge, covering the
ends of the handles and the button loop.

DESIGN SECRETS UNRAVELLED...
This colourway is great for evening, but you could
turn this into an everyday bag by using different
yarns. A tweed wool could be contrasted with a
frothy bouclé, while a matte grey contrasted with
a shiny grey would be great for the office. You
could decorate the bag with old bead necklaces
or a collection of special buttons, or look out for
unusual braids or upholstery trimmings such as
bullion fringes or tassels.

always the bridesmaid

This beautiful bag would be ideal for bridesmaids, or even for the bride herself. It is soft, feminine and classy, with a touch of sparkle. The simple stockinette stitch is worked in stripes of contrasting textures.

MEASUREMENTS

Finished bag measures 8in (20.5cm) wide and 9in (23cm) high

GATHER TOGETHER…

Materials

A 1 x 1¾oz (50g) ball of light-weight (DK) wool/cotton mix yarn (123yd/113m per ball) in cream
B 1 x ⅞oz (25g) ball of medium-weight (aran) velour (velvet)-style tape (63yd/58m per ball) in cream
C 1 x 1¾oz (50g) ball of medium-weight (aran) cotton mix bouclé yarn (136yd/125m per ball) in cream
D 1 x 1¾oz (50g) ball of light-weight (DK) mohair/metallic mix yarn (174yd/190m per ball) in cream

Needles and notions

1 pair of size 6 (4mm) needles
24in (61cm) of ½in (1.5cm)-wide satin ribbon for handles
selection of cream seed beads and ¼in (0.5cm) beads
six 10in (25.5cm) lengths of ¼in (0.5cm)-wide cream ribbons for threading through bag and beads, and two 10in (25.5cm) of ½in (1.5cm) wide cream ribbons
Lining fabric 20in (51cm) x 12in (30.5cm)

GAUGE

22 sts and 28 rows to 4in (10cm) measured over st st using size 6 (4mm) needles and yarn A

Knit note: Two strands of yarn D are used together. Make sure that you work through both strands for each stitch.

Knit your bag…

Front and back (work 2 the same)
Using size 6 (4mm) needles and A, cast on 44 sts.
Using A, work 12 rows in st st (1 row k, 1 row p), starting with a k row.
Using B, work 16 rows.
Using C, work 8 rows.
Using A, work 10 rows.
Using D, work 12 rows.
Using C, work in st st until front measures 8½in (21.5cm) from beg, ending with a k row.
Using C, knit 3 rows.
Bind off purlwise.

to finish…

Press according to instructions on ball bands. Make a simple lining as shown on pages 114–115. Decorate front only with ribbons and beads. Sew on two pieces of wide ribbon between stripes. Add beads as desired. Use the thinner ribbon to weave in and out of the knitted fabric. Add large beads by bringing the ribbon to RS, threading on a bead and taking the ribbon back to the WS. Join side and base seams. Cut two 12in (30.5cm) lengths of wide ribbon for the handles. Attach each end of handle 2in (5cm) in from side seam. With WS together, slip the lining into the bag and slipstitch into place below the bound-off edge, covering the ends of the handles.

DESIGN SECRETS UNRAVELLED…

Don't just think weddings for this glamorous bag. You could knit one for the evening using chenilles, silks and metallics in deep, rich shades of red. Or you could make a summer version in light cottons, silks and ribbons in pastel shades of pink. To be really frivolous, mix different fashion yarns together; fake furs, eyelash yarns, yarns with multi-coloured slubs and slinky ribbons – just keep a common colour running through all of them.

YARN FOCUS

Yarns are available in many tempting textures, and the colour ranges almost always include cream. Some are a whiter shade than others, some are buttery, and many are somewhere in between. Here, I collected together a range of shades and textures in roughly the same light-weight (DK) thickness. I love the contrast of the matte velour yarn with the sparkle in the mohair and the smoothness of the wool with the fun of the bouclé.

MEASUREMENTS
Finished bag measures 8in (20.5cm) wide
and 9in (23cm) high

GATHER TOGETHER...
Materials
A 2 x 1¾oz (50g) balls of light-weight (DK) cotton
mix yarn (98yd/90m per ball) in fern green
B 1 x 1¾oz (50g) ball of medium-weight (aran)
silk/cotton-mix tweed yarn (118yd/108m per ball)
in dark red

Needles and notions
1 pair of size 8 (5mm) needles
1 pair of size 6 (4mm) needles
Lining fabric 20in (51cm) x 12in (30.5cm)

GAUGE
17 sts and 24 rows to 4in (10cm) measured over
st st using size 8 (5mm) needles and yarn A

YARN FOCUS
The yarn for the roses is a silk/cotton mix that I
love for its dry handle. The yarn is medium-weight
(aran) to create a really thick fabric that rolls up
into the fantastic roses. I wanted a smooth yarn to
contrast with this, so chose a thick cotton yarn with
enough body to hold the weight of the roses.

DESIGN SECRETS UNRAVELLED...
For a totally different look, you could use warm
tweed wools for the roses and bag and knit the
leaves in a contrasting shiny ribbon yarn. Or, for a
delicate version, you could try a soft mohair-mix
yarn for the roses set against a silk bag. Use red,
bright pink, soft pink or deep purple for the roses,
and keep the bag dark green or use a lively bright
green instead. You could also use this green for the
leaves and introduce a third colour for the bag itself.

Make a bold statement with these stunning three-dimensional knitted roses;
the basic bag is transformed from its simplicity and made into something
unique. The roses are knitted in stockinette stitch with one row of simple
decreasing (k2tog) to shape them. The leaves are shaped using yarn overs,
k2tog, ssk and sk2po (see pages 105–107). A smaller rose is used with a loop
to form a simple fastening.

Knit your bag...
Front and back (work 2 the same)
Using size 8 (5mm) needles and A, cast on 34 sts.
Work in st st (1 row k, 1 row p), starting with a k
row, until front measures 8½in (21.5cm) from beg,
ending with a k row.
Knit 3 rows.
Bind off purlwise.

Handles (make 2)
Using size 8 (5mm) needles and A, cast on 51 sts.
Work 4 rows in st st.
Bind off.

Roses (make 6)
Using size 6 (4mm) needles and B, cast on 40 sts.
Work 6 rows in st st, starting with a k row.
Next Row (K2tog) 20 times. 20 sts.
Purl 1 row.
Bind off. Cut yarn leaving a long length for sewing
on to bag. Roll the bound-off edge around to form
the rose. Roll some tightly and others more loosely.
Secure with a few stitches through all thicknesses
at the base.

Rose fastening
Using size 6 (4mm) needles and B, cast on 20 sts.
Work 4 rows in st st, starting with a k row.
Next Row (K2tog) 10 times. 10 sts.
Purl 1 row.
Bind off. Cut yarn leaving a long length for sewing
onto bag. Roll the bound-off edge around tightly to
form the rose. Secure with a few stitches through
all thicknesses at the base.

Leaves (make 5)
Using size 8 (5mm) needles and A, cast on 3 sts
and purl 1 row.
Row 1 RS K1, yfwd, k1, yfwd, k1. 5 sts.
Row 2 and every foll WS row Purl.
Row 3 K2, yfwd, k1, yfwd, k2. 7 sts.
Row 5 K3, yfwd, k1, yfwd, k3. 9 sts.
Row 7 Ssk, k5, k2tog. 7 sts.
Row 9 Ssk, k3, k2tog. 5 sts.
Row 11 Ssk, k1, k2tog. 3 sts.
Row 13 Sk2po. 1 st.
Cut yarn, leaving a long length for sewing onto bag,
and thread through rem st.

to finish...
Press front and back according to instructions on
ball band. Make a simple lining as shown on pages
114–115. Sew the roses onto the front, sewing
around the base. Lay the rose towards the top of
the bag and secure with a few stitches. Sew on the
leaves between the roses. Sew the smaller rose
fastening in the centre of the front just below the
g st edging. Join the side and base seams. Sew on
the handles, making sure they are central, with the
rev st st side facing out.

Loop
Using size 6 (4mm) needles and A, cast on 30 sts.
Bind off.

Sew the loop to the inside of the back in the centre.
With WS together, slip the lining into the bag and
slipstitch into place below the bound-off edge,
covering the ends of the handles and loop.

in a flap

MEASUREMENTS

Finished bag measures 8in (20.5cm) wide
and 9in (23cm) high

GATHER TOGETHER...
Materials

1 x 3½oz (100g) ball of medium-weight
(aran) wool tweed yarn (175yd/160m per ball)
in blue-green

1 x ⅞oz (25g) ball of super-fine-weight mohair/
silk mix yarn (229yd/210m per ball) in jade

Needles and notions

1 pair of size 10½ (7mm) needles
1 pair of size 10 (6mm) needles
Large button or brooch

GAUGE

12 sts and 18 rows to 4in (10cm) measured over
st st using size 10½ (7mm) needles and one
strand of yarn A and two strands of yarn B
held together

*Knit note: One strand of yarn A and two strands
of yarn B are used together to make a thicker
yarn. Make sure that you work through all three
strands for each stitch.*

YARN FOCUS

I used a mix of yarns for this bag: a tweed wool
and a soft mohair yarn. Together they make up a
bulky-weight (chunky) yarn. I wanted to achieve
a mix of textures but kept each yarn in the same
colour family – blue-greens. A vintage brooch used
as a button adds an eye-catching touch of sparkle
to an otherwise robust and woolly bag.

---

*This version of the basic pattern has the addition of a closing flap and a
practical shoulder strap. The flap is knitted in garter stitch so will lie flat rather
than curling up, and the same stitch is used for the strap.*

Knit your bag...
Front

Using size 10½ (7mm) needles, cast on 24 sts.
Work in st st (1 row k, 1 row p), starting with a k
row, until front measures 8½in (21.5cm) from beg,
ending with a k row. **
Knit 3 rows.
Bind off purlwise.

Back

Work as given for Front to **.

Shape flap

Work 15 rows in g st (every row k).
Dec 1 st at end of next and every foll alt row
to 4 sts, ending with a WS row.
Button Loop Row Bind off 3 sts, cast on 8 sts.
Bind off loosely.

Strap

Using size 10 (6mm) needles, cast on 5 sts
and work in g st for 40in (101.5cm).
Bind off.

To finish...

Join side and base seams. Sew ends of strap
onto each side of back at top. Sew end of button
loop down. Fold flap over as if to close bag, mark
position of button. Sew on button.

DESIGN SECRETS UNRAVELLED...

Mixing yarns together means that you can create
your own unique yarn. It's also an innovative way
of using up oddments of yarn or thin yarn that
you wouldn't normally use. To get a bulky-weight
(chunky) yarn, try mixing three light-weight (DK)
yarns together, such as a metallic and tweeds,
or a medium-weight (aran) and a light-weight
(DK), like a smooth cotton and a bouclé. Use more
strands of thinner yarns. Keep them in the same
colour group or put a contrasting colour into the
mix – add a gold into a mix of greens, or purple
into blues.

patching it up

This is a delightfully colourful and quirky bag that lets you run riot with texture and details. It's also a useful size – big enough to carry around notebooks and sketchbooks if inspiration seizes you while you're out and about. The addition of the beads, buttons and charms lets you add extra individual details – you could make the bag extra-special by using things that have meaning for you, such as favourite pieces of old costume jewellery, or thrift-shop treasures. This is a fun and playful piece, so let your imagination run wild.

Sew on special beads, favourite buttons, and vintage charms to give this bag extra interest and individuality.

DESIGN SECRETS UNRAVELLED...
I used a limited colour palette here, but this bag would be an ideal way to use up any oddments of yarn that you have. Collect together a range of blues, or greens, or pinks in as many textures as you can. It doesn't matter if you put wool next to cotton, or silk with mohair. Alternatively, you could knit each strip in a different colour for exciting contrasts.

YARN FOCUS
I put shades of fresh aqua and rich raspberry together as they contrast well with each other. With this simple colour choice, I collected several yarns of different textures; a dry cotton/silk mix, a crisp mercerized cotton, a luxurious mohair and an alpaca/silk mix. Each texture shows the colours off differently.

patching it up

MEASUREMENTS

11in (28cm) wide and 13½in (34.5cm) long

GATHER TOGETHER...
Materials

A 1 x 1¾oz (50g) ball of light-weight (DK) cotton/
silk mix (218yd/200m per ball) in pale aqua

B 1 x ⅞oz (25g) ball of super-fine-weight (2ply)
mohair yarn (229yd/210m per ball)
in dark raspberry

C 1 x 1¾oz (50g) ball of light-weight (DK) cotton
(115yd/106m per ball) in raspberry

D 1 x 1¾oz (50g) ball of medium-weight (aran)
cotton/angora mix yarn (98yd/90m per ball)
in aqua

E 2 x 1¾oz (50g) balls of light-weight (DK)
alpaca/silk mix yarn (114yd/105m per ball)
in raspberry

Needles and notions

1 pair of size 7 (4.5mm) needles
Button for fastening
Selection of buttons, charms and large beads for
embellishments
Lining fabric 24½in (62cm) x 14¾in (37.5cm)

GAUGE

18 sts and 24 rows to 4in (10cm) measured over
st st (1 row k, 1 row p) using size 7 (4.5mm)
needles and 2 strands of C

*Knit note: Yarns A, C and E use two strands
together throughout. Use three strands of B
together throughout. Make sure that you work
through all strands for each stitch.*

The front of this colourful patchwork bag is made up of strips of stockinette stitch woven together; each strip is worked in a different texture or colour. The back is knitted in one piece in stripes. After weaving the strip for the front, the pieces are sewn together and secured further by adding various buttons, charms and large beads. The handles are knitted in garter stitch, and a single button and loop provides the fastening.

Knit your bag...
Front
Vertical strips

Using size 7 (4.5mm) needles, yarn and number of cast-on sts as indicated, work 13½in (34.5cm) in st st (1 row k, 1 row p), starting with a k row and ending with a p row as follows:

Strip 1 Use 2 strands of A and cast on 8 sts.
Strip 2 Use 3 strands of B and cast on 10 sts.
Strip 3 Use 2 strands of C and cast on 6 sts.
Strip 4 Use 1 strand of D and cast on 12 sts.
Strip 5 Use 2 strands of A and cast on 6 sts.
Strip 6 Use 2 strands of C and cast on 10 sts.

Horizontal strips

Using size 7 (4.5mm) needles, yarn and number of cast-on sts as indicated, work 11in (28cm) in st st, starting with a k row and ending with a p row as follows:

Strip 1 Use 2 strands of E and cast on 12 sts.
Strip 2 Use 2 strands of C and cast on 10 sts.
Strip 3 Use 2 strands of A and cast on 14 sts.
Strip 4 Use 3 strands of B and cast on 8 sts.
Strip 5 Use 2 strands of E and cast on 10 sts.
Strip 6 Use 1 strand of D and cast on 10 sts.

Back

Using size 7 (4.5mm) needles and 2 strands of C, cast on 49 sts.
Using C, work 19 rows in st st, starting with a k row.
Using 2 strands of E, work 8 rows.
Using 2 strands of A, work 4 rows.
Using 3 strands of B, work 10 rows.
Using 1 strand of D, work 8 rows.
Rep this stripe sequence until back measures 12½in (32cm) from beg, ending with a p row.
Using 2 strands of C, knit 5 rows.
Bind off.

Handles (make 2)

Using size 7 (4.5mm) needles and 2 strands of C, cast on 108 sts.
Knit 3 rows.
Bind off.

to finish...

Sew in all ends neatly. Press according to instructions on ball bands, making sure the edges of the strips are lying flat.

Lining

Use the back to make a simple lining (see pages 114–115). On a flat surface, lay vertical strips in order next to each other. Weave the horizontal strips alternately under and over the verticals. Sew together around the outside edge, making sure the ends are level and corners are square. In some places where the strips cross over each other, sew a square of small running stitches to secure in a contrasting or matching yarn. Do this often enough so that the strips lay securely next to each and will not move. Sew on selection of buttons and charms. Place back and front together with WS together. Sew around sides and base using a small running stitch. Sew fastening button in centre of front 1in (2.5cm) below top edge. Using 2 strands of C, make a fastening loop in the centre of the back on the top edge. Work buttonhole stitch evenly around the loop (see page 120). Sew on handles. With WS together, slip the lining into the bag and slipstitch neatly into place around top of bag, covering the ends of the handles.

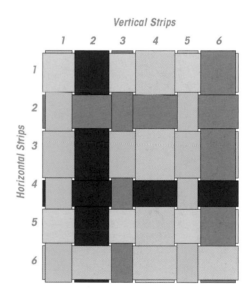

off the cuff

This crisp and smart-looking bag is ideal for taking to the office or for any occasion when you need to look the business. The bag takes its inspiration from city suits, recreating a classic pinstripe fabric in a high-quality yarn with a glamorous accent of metallic thread. The three buttons echo the cuff detail of a smart suit. The rose corsage offers a little feminine contrast and colour. It is detachable – so you can take it off and wear it in your lapel buttonhole once you get to work.

DESIGN SECRETS UNRAVELLED...

This bag would look sensational worked in dark purple silk with a contrasting crisp metallic gold for evening. For a summer version, candy stripes would be fun and feminine. For winter, you could use a tweed wool with a contrasting mohair stripe. Instead of using a different yarn for the stripe, you could simply use the same yarn in a different colour. You could also experiment with the size and colour of the buttons.

YARN FOCUS

I wanted a sober grey for this fabric, and chose a luxury cashmere-mix yarn. I could have put a plain white stripe into it but instead used a silver-grey metallic thread. This takes the bag from being a straight copy of a pinstripe fabric and adds an unconventional touch to a classic design. I worked the rose corsage in dark red and dark green, which fitted in with the sophisticated tailored look.

off the cuff

MEASUREMENTS

Finished bag measures 10in (25cm) wide
at base and 8in (20.5cm) high and
2in (5cm) deep at base

GATHER TOGETHER...
Materials

A 2 x 1¾oz (50g) balls of light-weight (DK) wool/
cashmere-mix yarn (142yd/130m per ball) in grey

B 2 x ⅞oz (25g) balls of fine-weight (4ply)
metallic yarn (218yd/200m per ball) in silver

Needles and notions

1 pair of size 6 (4mm) needles
Pair of clear plastic bag handles 6in (15cm)
wide at base
Lining fabric 25in (63.5cm) x 15in (38cm)
17in (43cm) of ¼in (7mm) wide ribbon
3 buttons
Thick card for base

GAUGE

22 sts and 30 rows to 4in (10cm) measured over
st st using size 6 (4mm) needles and yarn A

Knit note: *Use two strands of yarn B together
throughout. Make sure that you work through both
strands for each stitch.*

The pinstripe effect of this classy bag is easily achieved by knitting the bag
from side to side instead of from the base upwards. The flared shape is worked
by casting on stitches and then binding them off on the opposite side seam.
A clear plastic handle is attached with ribbon, which is also used for the button
fastening. The flat base is strengthened with a removable insert of thick card.

Knit your bag...

(The bag is knitted in one piece from side seam to
side seam.)
Using size 6 (4mm) needles and A, cast on 33 sts
and purl 1 row.

Shape sides

Work 14 rows in st st (1 row k, 1 row p), starting
with a k row, cast on 4 sts at beg of every row in
stripe pattern of 3 rows A, 1 row B, 6 rows A, 1 row B
and 3 rows A. 89 sts.
Using A, cast on 7 sts at beg of foll 2 rows. 103 sts.
Next Row Using A, k2, p1, k to last 3 sts, p1, k2.
Next Row Using B, p2, k1, p to last 3 sts, k1, p2.
These 2 rows set the fold-line on the top edges.
Working in stripe pattern of 6 rows A and 1 row B,
work 52 more rows as set.

Shape sides

Keeping stripe pattern correct, cast off 7 sts at beg
of next 2 rows and cast off 4 sts at beg of every foll
row to 33 sts. Bind off.

to finish...

Sew in all ends. Pin the bag out so it measures
12in (30.5cm) long at centre between cast-on and
bound-off edges and 18¾in (47.5cm) at widest
point. Press according to instructions on ball band.

Lining

Make a lining with a flat base (see pages
115–116).

Base

Cut a piece of thick card 10in (25.5cm) long and
2in (5cm) wide. Make a base as shown on page
116. Join the side seams of the bag. To form the
bottom corners, turn the bag inside out. Place side
seam along fold-line at base and place a marker
1in (2.5cm) down from point. Sew across corner at
right angles. Fold corner along base and sew into
position. Turn the facing at the top to the WS and
slipstitch into position.

Attaching handles

Cut four pieces of ribbon 3in (7.5cm) long. Thread
each piece through a hole on the handles and fold
in half. Tack through both thicknesses to hold in
position. Pin the handles into place, making sure
that they are centralized (use the stripe pattern as
a guide). Sew the ribbons securely to the facing,
making sure the stitching is below the fold-line.

Fastening loop

Cut a piece of ribbon 5in (12.5cm) long. Fold
in half and sew each end onto the facing in the
centre, making sure the stitches are below the fold-
line. Fold the loop over as if to close the bag and
mark the position of the first button. Sew on three
buttons, equally spaced.

With WS together, slip the lining into the bag and
slipstitch neatly into place onto the back facing,
covering the ends of the ribbons. Push base into
bag so that it lies flat.

MEASUREMENTS
Rose measures approx 2in (5cm) in diameter

GATHER TOGETHER...
Materials
Oddments of dark red (A) and dark green (B)
light-weight (DK) wool yarn

Needles and notions
1 pair of size 3 (3.25mm) needles
Brooch pin

GAUGE
Gauge is not so important for this project; the
chances are, if you have the gauge correct for the
bag you should be fine with the corsage

YARN FOCUS
I wanted this rose to be three-dimensional so
chose a light-weight (DK) wool. It has enough
body to form thick petals that stand apart from
each other, but will still roll to form a natural
soft edge. The deep red and dark green make a
stunning classic rose.

This simple corsage offers a sophisticated feminine accent to the snappy
colours of the bag. The leaves of the corsage are shaped using a variety of
increases and decreases: yo, ssk, k2tog and sk2po. See pages 105–107 for
detailed instructions on these techniques.

Knit your corsage...
Rose
Using size 3 (3.25mm) needles and A,
cast on 8 sts.
Work 10 rows in st st, starting with a k row.
**Next Row Bind off 6 sts, cast on 6 sts. 8 sts.
Work 10 rows in st st.
Rep from ** 7 times more.
Bind off.

Leaves (make 2)
Using size 3 (3.25mm) needles and B, cast
on 3 sts and purl 1 row.
Row 1 RS K1, yfwd, k1, yfwd, k1. 5 sts.
Row 2 and every foll WS row Purl.
Row 3 K2, yfwd, k1, yfwd, k2. 7 sts.
Row 5 K3, yfwd, k1, yfwd, k3. 9 sts.
Row 7 Ssk, k5, k2tog. 7 sts.
Row 9 Ssk, k3, k2tog. 5 sts.
Row 11 Ssk, k1, k2tog. 3 sts.
Row 13 Sk2po.
Cut yarn and thread through rem st.

to finish...
Do not press rose or leaves. Form the rose by
rolling it up from the centre out. Join with a few
stitches through all thicknesses at the base. Sew
the two leaves on either side at the base. Sew on
the brooch pin. Attach to bag.

DESIGN SECRETS UNRAVELLED...
Because this rose uses so little yarn, it is
an ideal way to use up any oddments of yarn
that you have. It doesn't take long to make so
you could knit several to try out different yarn
combinations before going on to a bigger project.
Try this rose in a lighter colour, such as pale
peach or dusty pink, for a more romantic bloom.
Worked in silk, it would be more lustrous and
fall into a softer form. You could use a mohair-
mix yarn for the rose and contrast it with a shiny
viscose ribbon for the leaves.

classy convertibles

Backpacks are fantastically practical; they leave your hands free, are easy and comfortable to carry and are usefully roomy. But practicality doesn't preclude stylishness, and backpacks can work equally well for a city chic or a weekend casual look. This one has an ingenious secret, too; it can be converted into a shoulder bag simply by buttoning the straps in a different way, see Secret Life shoulder bag (pages 40–41). You will no longer have to choose between a practical backpack and shoulder bag chic!

This versatile backpack can quickly be converted into a sophisticated shoulder bag by simply unbuttoning the straps.

DESIGN SECRETS UNRAVELLED...
This backpack would look wonderfully fresh worked in cotton for a summer beach bag. You could use matte cotton in denim blue or in natural linen to create a classic look. Add an individual touch by sewing beads or shells on the pocket. For a winter version, you could try a bouclé yarn or Icelandic Lopi for a thick, robust fabric, or a fantastic rich tweed wool for depth of colour.

YARN FOCUS
Plain stockinette stitch is the ideal fabric for showing off a self-striping or multi-coloured yarn. I chose this one because it has texture as well as colour; it features slubs of bright colour, twists of silk threads and the softness of wool. I used one ball at a time (manufacturers usually recommend using two balls alternately), as I wanted to emphasize the stripes and changes of colour.

get back backpack

MEASUREMENTS
Backpack measures 12in (30.5cm) long,
12in (30.5cm) at widest point and 4in (10cm)
deep at base

GATHER TOGETHER...
Materials
4 x 1¾oz (50g) balls of medium-weight (aran)
self-striping wool-mix yarn (95yd/87m per hank)
in blue/purple/green

Needles and notions
1 pair of size 7 (4.5mm) needles
Stitch markers
14 1in (2.5cm) flat buttons

GAUGE
15 sts and 22 rows to 4in (10cm) measured
over st st (1 row k, 1 row p) using
size 7 (4.5mm) needles

The flared shape of this wonderfully textural bag is achieved by decreasing stitches on each edge. The flap is picked up from the back and continues the acute shape. The straps are worked in seed (UK: moss) stitch; this is a robust stitch that will lay nice and flat and keep its shape. There's a roomy pocket on the front for another practical touch.

Knit your bag...

Back
Using size 7 (4.5mm) needles, cast on 45 sts and work 12 rows in st st (1 row k, 1 row p) starting with a k row.
Cast on 8 sts at beg of next 2 rows. 61 sts.
Cont in st st, dec 1 st at each end of every foll 5th row to 35 sts.
Place markers on the 2nd and 34th sts of the last row.
Next Row K1, *p1, k1; rep from * to end.
This row forms seed (UK: moss) stitch.
Work 3 more rows in seed (UK: moss) stitch.
Bind off in patt.

Front
Work as given for Back, omitting markers.

Flap
With RS of work facing and using size 7 (4.5mm) needles, pick up and k 33 sts between markers on Back.
Next Row WS (K1, p1) twice, k1, p to last 5 sts, (k1, P1) twice, k1.
Next Row (K1, p1) twice, k to last 4 sts, (p1, k1) twice.
These 2 rows set seed (UK: moss) stitch borders and st st.
Patt 7 more rows.
** **Dec Row RS** (K1, p1) twice, ssk, k to last 6 sts, k2tog, (p1, k1) twice.

Patt 4 rows.
Dec Row WS (K1, p1) twice, k2tog, p to last 6 sts, ssk, (p1, k1) twice.
Patt 4 rows.
Rep from ** twice more. 21 sts.
Dec Row RS (K1, p1) twice, ssk, k to last 6 sts, k2tog, (p1, k1) twice.
Patt 1 row.
Buttonhole Row (K1, p1) 4 times, k1, yo, k2tog, (p1, k1) 4 times.
Work 3 rows in seed (UK: moss) stitch.
Bind off in patt.

Pocket
Using size 7 (4.5mm) needles, cast on 23 sts and work 4 rows in st st, starting with a k row.
Cast on 3 sts at beg of next 2 rows. 29 sts.
Cont in st st until pocket measures 4½in (11.5cm) from beg, ending with a k row.
Work 4 rows in seed (UK: moss) stitch.
Bind off in patt.

Pocket flap
Using size 7 (4.5mm) needles, cast on 23 sts and work 3 rows in seed (UK: moss) stitch.
Buttonhole Row Patt 5, yo, k2tog, patt to last 6 sts, yo, k2tog, patt 4.
Patt 1 row.
Next Row RS (K1, p1) twice, k to last 4 sts, (p1, k1) twice.
Next Row K1, p1, k1, p to last 3 sts, k1, p1, k1.

Rep these 2 rows until pocket flap measures
3in (7.5cm) from beg.
Bind off.

Straps (make 2)
Using size 7 (4.5mm) needles, cast on 5 sts.
Work 4 rows in seed (UK: moss) stitch.
Buttonhole Row K1, p1, yo, k2tog, k1.
Patt 9 rows.
Work Buttonhole Row once more.
Rep last 10 rows once more.
Cont in seed (UK: moss) stitch until strap measures
29in (74cm) from beg.
Bind off in patt.

to finish...

Sew in all ends. Press according to instructions on
ball band. Join corner seams of pocket. Place a
marker in centre stitch of front 3in (7.5cm) above
cast-on edge. Count 11 stitches each side of this
centre stitch and place markers. Sew pocket in
place between these markers. Sew pocket flap
above pocket so seam is hidden when flap is
folded over. Sew buttons onto pocket to match
buttonholes. Join base and side seams. Place
side seam along base seam and join corner
seams. Turn backpack over so back is facing with
flap at top. Lay one strap upside-down onto back
so the end without buttonholes is 1in (2.5cm)
below flap and the strap is lined up with the edge
of the flap. Sew securely in place. Sew on other
strap onto the opposite side. Using the buttonholes
on the strap as a guide for spacing, sew three
buttons onto the back in a line up from each
corner and three buttons onto RS of each strap at
the top. Button ends of straps to buttons at base,
adjusting the length as required by using three,
two or one buttons. Convert the backpack into a
shoulder bag (see pages 40–41).

*The use of self-striping yarn for this backpack
takes the hard work out of creating something
so delightfully colourful. The chunky buttons
add another fun detail.*

secret life shoulder bag

MEASUREMENTS

Shoulder bag measures 12in (30.5cm) long,
12in (30.5cm) at widest point and 4in (10cm)
deep at base

GATHER TOGETHER...
Materials

A 4 x 1¾oz (50g) balls of medium-weight (aran)
bouclé wool-mix yarn (76yd/70m per ball)
in brown

B 3 x 1¾oz (50g) balls of light-weight (DK) wool
(131yd/120m per ball) in dark brown

Needles and notions

1 pair of size 7 (4.5mm) needles
14 1in (2.5cm) flat buttons

GAUGE

15 sts and 22 rows to 4in (10cm) measured over
st st (1 row k, 1 row p) using size 7 (4.5mm)
needles and yarns A and B held together

Knit note: Two yarns are used together to make
a thicker yarn. Make sure that you work through
both strands for each stitch.

There's something very satisfying about versatile bags, as with this backpack,
which can be restyled into a sophisticated shoulder bag just be rebuttoning
the shoulder straps. This version is just as roomy, and the attractive flared
shape is revealed more by omitting the pocket. The straps can be lengthened
or shortened according to use.

Knit your bag...
Back, Front, Flap and Straps

Work as given for the Get Back Backpack, using
yarns A and B held together.

to finish...

Work as given for backpack. For a simpler finish,
you could omit the pocket as I've done here.

To use as a shoulder bag, twist one strap and
button it to the other with the top buttons,
adjusting length as required by using three, two
or one buttons. Twist second strap and button
to top buttons.

YARN FOCUS

The bag isn't lined, so I needed to use a thick
fabric for the bag to hold its shape. I wanted to
use an astrakhan-style yarn, but found it was too
soft on its own. By mixing it with a light-weight
(DK) wool, I produced a fabric that is wonderfully
dense and rich. The dark brown of the wool yarn
is punctuated with twists of the more chestnut-
coloured astrakhan yarn.

DESIGN SECRETS UNRAVELLED...

You can create a dense fabric by working a
thick yarn on smaller needles than those that
are recommended on the ball band. Use a bulky-
weight (chunky) yarn or make up a mix of yarns
to this weight. Knit a sample first and adjust your
needles to achieve the correct gauge. Try working
two textures together as I have done; use a
smooth wool with a slub yarn, or a slinky
ribbon with a thick-and-thin yarn.

*Think carefully about what buttons to
use; here I chose buttons with a lovely
sheen and lustre to stand out against
the dark, rich colour of the fabric.*

falling
leaves

This baguette-style bag has a delightfully neat, chic shape. It is made in a warm, cosy fabric produced from green tweed wool with slots of fiery colours worked in a contrasting stitch. The bag has been fulled, which produces a lovely dense texture. The contrasting colours are strong and yet subtle. This is a bag that is full of detail and interest while retaining an understated stylishness.

This bag has a wonderfully compact shape, and the design means you can really experiment with colour and tone.

DESIGN SECRETS UNRAVELLED...

If you are going to full the bag, you should use a 100% wool. It doesn't have to be tweed; you could also use a plain solid colour. Instead of using contrasting colours for the slots, you could try a complementary shade instead. Use blue for the main colour and green for the slots; or dark pink and light pink; or purple with mauve. You could also choose not to full the bag; the pattern stitch is so three-dimensional it works equally well unfulled. Knit it instead in a denim yarn, or linen for the summer.

YARN FOCUS

This beautiful green tweed wool has flecks of orange and yellow together with darker greens. These flecks inspired me to add slots of colour in fiery oranges; they contrast with the green but also add to the seasonal feel of the finished fabric. I used tapestry wools for the contrasting colours. If you're using only a small amount of colour, tapestry wools are ideal. They are available in such a wide range of colours that I knew I would be able to get a good choice of oranges and rusts.

falling leaves

MEASUREMENTS

Before fulling – 12½in (32cm) wide and
6½in (16.5cm) long from base to zip
After fulling – 11½in (29cm) wide and
6in (15cm) long

GATHER TOGETHER...
Materials

A 2 x 1¾oz (50g) balls of light-weight (DK) tweed
wool (123yd/113m per ball) in green with orange
and yellow flecks
B 6 x 8m skeins of tapestry wool in dark ginger,
orange, light orange, dark yellow-orange, rust,
light rust

Needles and notions

Size 6 (4mm) 24in (60cm)-long circular needles
1 pair of size 6 (4mm) needles
Stitch markers
Zip – measure length of opening after fulling

GAUGE

20 sts and 28 rows to 4in (10cm) measured
over st st using size 6 (4mm) needles

Special abbreviations

sl2(4) wyib   slip 2 (4) sts purlwise with yarn
at back of work

---

*Knit note: B is used to indicate the contrasting
colours. Use one for each set of 4 patt rounds,
choosing them randomly. When slipping stitches,
carry the yarn loosely across the back of the
work. Do not pull tight.*

The stitch pattern used for this bag is blind buttonhole stitch (full instructions
for this are given below). This is a great way to introduce colour and texture
without having to work with more than one yarn at a time. The bag is knitted
on circular needles, transferring to flat knitting for the shaping at the top edges.
The curved edge is made by binding off and decreasing stitches. The bag is
closed with a zip, inserted after fulling (see page 111).

Knit your bag...

Back and Front (worked in one piece)
Using size 6 (4mm) circular needles and A,
cast on 128 sts.
Spread the stitches evenly around the needle,
making sure the cast-on edge faces inward and
is not twisted. Place a marker on the right-hand
needle (this indicates the beginning of each round
and is slipped on every round), bring the two
needles together and purl the first st on the
left-hand needle, pulling up the yarn to prevent
a gap. Continue purling each cast-on st to reach
the marker.
Purl 9 more rows.
Commence blind buttonhole st.
**Round 1 Using B, k2, sl4 wyib, *k4, sl4 wyib;
rep from * to last 2 sts, k2.
Rep this round 3 times more.
Round 5 Using A, k2, p4, *k4, p4; rep from * to last
2 sts, k2.
Using A, p 3 rounds.
Round 9 Using B, sl2 wyib, k4, *sl4 wyib, k4;
rep from * to last 2 sts, sl2 wyib.
Rep this round 3 times more.
Round 13 Using A, p2, k4, *p4, k4; rep from * to
last 2 sts, p2.
Using A, p 3 rounds.****
Rep from ** to ** twice more.

Shape top

Next Round P24, bind off 16 sts, p48 (including last st used in binding off), bind off 16 sts, p24, remove marker, p24 and turn.

From now on use the circular needle as you would straight needles – working backwards and forwards, turning at the end of each row.

**Working on the first set of 48 sts, bind off 6 sts at beg of next 2 rows, and 5 sts at beg of foll 2 rows. Place markers at each end of last row.

Bind off 4 sts at beg of next 2 rows. 18 sts.

Dec 1 st at each end of every row to 8 sts, ending with a p row.

Bind off.

With RS of work facing, rejoin yarn to rem 48 sts and p to end, turn.

Work as given for first side from **.

Strap

Using size 6 (4mm) needles and A, cast on 10 sts. Work 24in (61cm) in st st (1 row k, 1 row p), ending with a p row.

Bind off.

To finish...

Sew in all ends. Lay bag flat, with beginning of cast-on edge at one side. Place a marker at the opposite fold for other side seam. Join base seam. To create the flat base, push the corners in and, on the WS, sew across the point 1in (2.5cm) from the tip. Join curved edges together from bound-off sts down to markers.

Fulling

Read the instructions on page 111. Turn the bag inside out. To keep some of the depth of the blind buttonhole stitch, full the bag until the stitches just begin to mesh together. Keep pulling the strands of B away from the background fabric. Full the strap more so that the stitches disappear and the fabric becomes fuzzy. Keep pulling the edges out so they don't roll together. Dry as instructed, pushing a thin mould into the bag to give it a box shape.

Measure the handle cut to the desired length plus 2in (5cm) from overlaps (fulled fabric won't unravel once cut). My strap is 20in (51cm) finished length. Place one end on the side of the bag on the RS. Sew into place. Sew on the other end to match. Sew in the zip along the curved edges (see page 117).

lacy
lovelies

This pretty, feminine bag is just the thing for a special occasion. It can be knitted in a cream cotton yarn to carry on a hot summer's day, or transformed into a glamourous bag for the evening, simply by changing the colour and shoulder strap (see page 49). The beauty and delicacy of lace may not seem to lend itself to bags, which tend to get a lot of wear and tear. However, the introduction of a lining gives the bag sufficient robustness to make it usable, while also serving to make the intricacy and openness of the lace stitches stand out more. These bags are ideal if you are new to lace knitting; they aren't very big, so will take no time to knit.

Create a sophisticated evening version of this bag by simply using a darker, more glamorous colour and swapping the knitted cord for a silky ribbon shoulder strap.

DESIGN SECRETS UNRAVELLED...

An important factor here is the colour of the lining, which is used as a facing to highlight the holes in the lace. The colour of the lace and the colour of the lining need to work effectively together. I thought the combination of cream and green would be very fresh for summer. For an alternative summer look, you could use a silk yarn in pale aqua with a raspberry lining or a linen yarn in natural terracotta faced with undyed linen fabric.

YARN FOCUS

Lace always looks effective worked in a crisp cotton yarn, so I chose a cream fine-weight (4ply). This thinner yarn means more stitches are cast on and more repeats of the lace are worked. The clean colour and crisp stitch definition allows the intricate lace pattern to be seen clearly. Alternatively, you can create a sophisticated evening look with a vibrant deep purple tweed wool, see page 49 for making up instructions.

summertime sweetie

MEASUREMENTS
Finished bag measures 20in (51cm) in
circumference and 9in (23cm) high

GATHER TOGETHER...
Materials
1 x 3½oz (100g) ball of fine-weight (4ply)
cotton yarn (370yd/338m per ball) in cream

Needles and notions
1 pair of size 3 (3.25mm) needles
2 size 3 (3.25mm) double-pointed needles
Lining fabric 24in (61cm) x 10in (25.5cm)

GAUGE
2 repeats of lace pattern (29 sts) measure 3½in
(9cm) using size 3 (3.25mm) needles; 32 rows to
4in (10cm) measured over lace pattern

This bag is worked in an easy lace pattern with an eight-row repeat. The large holes are made by throwing three yarn overs (yo – see page 106) around the needle and then working five stitches into it. The smaller holes are worked into two yarn overs and one yarn over. The lace is worked only on the sides of the bag; stitches are picked up and then decreased to form a flat circular base.

Knit your bag...
Using size 3 (3.25mm) needles, cast on 169 sts loosely and purl 1 row.

Row 1 RS K1, *ssk, k9, k2tog, k1; rep from * to end. 145 sts.

Row 2 P1, *p2tog, p7, ssp, p1; rep from * to end. 121 sts.

Row 3 K1, *ssk, k2, (yo) 3 times, k3, k2tog, k1; rep from * to end. 133 sts.

Row 4 P1, *p2tog, p2, (k1, p1, k1, p1, k1) into 3-yos, p1, ssp, p1; rep from * to end. 133 sts.

Row 5 K1, *ssk, k6, k2tog, k1; rep from * to end. 109 sts.

Row 6 P1, *p2tog, p7; rep from * to end. 97 sts.

Row 7 K1, *k2, yo, k1, (yo) twice, k1, (yo) twice, k1, yo, k3; rep from * to end. 169 sts.

Row 8 P1, *p2, p into yo, p1, (k1, p1) into 2-yos, p1, (k1, p1) into 2-yos, p1, p into yo, p2; rep from * to end. 169 sts.

These 8 rows form the lace pattern. Repeat these 8 rows 7 times more.
Knit 2 rows.

Picot Bind-Off Row Bind off 2 sts, *cast on 2 sts, bind off 5 sts; rep from * to end.

Sew in all ends. Using pins, stretch the bag out so it measures 20in (51cm) wide and 9in (23cm) high. Pin the bottom edge so that it is straight but leave the top edge in points. Gently steam, according to instructions on ball band. When the bag is dry, remove the pins.

Base
With RS of work facing and using size 3 (3.25mm) needles, pick up and knit 169 sts evenly around cast-on edge of bag.
Row 1 and every foll WS row Purl.

Row 2 K1, (ssk, k12) 12 times. 157 sts.
Row 4 K1, (ssk, k11) 12 times. 145 sts.
Row 6 K1, (ssk, K10) 12 times. 133 sts.
Row 8 K1, (ssk, k9) 12 times. 121 sts.
Cont to dec as set working 1 st less between each dec to 13 sts.
Cut yarn and thread through rem sts. Pull up tight and fasten off.

Drawstring/strap
Using size 3 (3.25mm) double-pointed needles, cast on 5 sts.
Knit 1 row. Do not turn the work but slide the sts to the other end of the needle. Pull up the yarn and knit the sts again. Repeat until cord measures 42in (106.5cm). Bind off. (See page 121 for more information on knitting cords.)

to finish...
Press the base according to instructions on ball band.

Lining
Cut a piece of lining fabric 9¼in (23.5cm) long by 23½in (59.5cm) wide. Make a hem on each side by folding in ⅞in (1.5cm) and then folding this over again. Tack the hems down temporarily by using large running stitches in a contrasting thread. Press and sew around each edge neatly. Remove tacking stitches. Place the RS of the lining onto the WS of the bag. Slipstitch the bottom of the lining to the cast-on edge and the top to the row at the beg of the 7th pattern repeat, leaving one st on each edge of the side seam free. Join side seam of bag. Slipstitch the lining side seam closed. Thread the cord through the large holes in the 7th pattern repeat. Join the ends of the cord.

MEASUREMENTS

Finished bag measures 20in (51cm) in circumference and 9in (23cm) high

GATHER TOGETHER...
Materials

3 x ⅞oz (25g) balls of fine-weight (4ply) wool tweed yarn (120yd/110m per ball) in purple

Needles and notions

1 pair of size 3 (3.25mm) needles
Lining fabric 24in (61cm) x 10in (25.5cm)
42in (106.5cm) of ⅞in (1.5cm)-wide satin ribbon

GAUGE

2 repeats of lace pattern (29 sts) measure 3½in (9cm) using size 3 (3.25mm) needles; 32 rows to 4in (10cm) measured over lace pattern

YARN FOCUS

To make an evening version of this bag, I chose a fantastic deep purple tweed wool, which alters the feel of the lace entirely. This really takes the lace pattern back to its roots, as it is an adaptation of a traditional Shetland lace shawl pattern used in shawl-making; I've added bigger holes to show off the wonderful silk fabric beneath.

This sophisticated evening version of the bag is knitted in the same way but is totally transformed through the choices of yarn and colour. To continue the glamourous evening theme, this bag is finished with a ribbon shoulder strap rather than a knitted cord.

Knit your bag...

Work as given for Summertime Sweetie, omitting the drawstring strap.

to finish...

Thread the ribbon through the large holes in the 7th pattern repeat. Sew the ends together.

DESIGN SECRETS UNRAVELLED...

Go for deep opulent colours for the evening version of the bag. Try a silk yarn in deep cranberry contrasted with a gold fabric for the lining. A rich matte blue chenille yarn would contrast wonderfully with a satin bronze lining.

The special binding-off technique used for this bag creates a picot edge – that is, the pointed tips around the top. This helps complete the delicate lacy look of the bag.

belt up bags

This is a funky and practical bag that is perfect for when you're rushing round town. The clever design means that the bag buttons onto your belt, leaving your hands free. The curved shape will fit snugly against you and the useful pockets are deep enough to carry your phone and your purse. Buttonholes on the straps allow the bag to be removed from the belt easily and cleverly converted into a relaxed-looking handbag (see pages 54–55).

The addition of the pockets to this useful bag are perfect for carrying your phone and all your other essential items.

YARN FOCUS

Sometimes you choose yarns for the colour; sometimes for the fibre (wool, cotton, silk and so on), and sometimes for the texture (eyelash, bouclé, slub and so on). I chose this yarn for the colour; I wanted a khaki green and this turned out to be the perfect shade. This yarn also has a grainy quality to it; the colour isn't solid, but contains high- and lowlights. As an alternative to the khaki green, I chose a sassy hot pink colour for the hands-free handbag (see pages 54–55), to create a softer, more feminine look.

DESIGN SECRETS UNRAVELLED...

You could work this bag in a denim yarn to go with your jeans; it will fade and age in the same way. But remember that some of these yarns shrink when washed, so your bag will be slightly smaller. Alternatively, knit it in sophisticated black or brown for a casually elegant look.

look, no hands!

MEASUREMENTS
Finished bag measures 9½in (24cm) wide
and 5½in (14cm) high from base to zip

GATHER TOGETHER...
Materials
3 x 1¾oz (50g) balls of light-weight (DK)
viscose/angora-mix yarn (137yd/125m per ball)
in khaki green

Needles and notions
1 pair of size 3 (3.25mm) needles
Stitch holder
Stitch markers
8in (20.5cm)-long zip
7 ¾in (2cm) diameter buttons

GAUGE
26 sts and 37 rows to 4in (10cm) measured
over st st using size 3 (3.25mm) needles

This funky-looking, tomboyish bag is perfect for a casual look. The body of the bag is worked in simple stockinette stitch; the addition of the pockets and the buttons lends it some visual interest, as well as increasing the practicality of the bag. Simple shaping gives the bag a curved edge that will fit well against your body. The addition of a zip (see page 117) means that your possessions will remain safely inside the bag while you run around town!

Knit your bag...

Back and Front (make 2 the same)
Using size 3 (3.25mm) needles, cast on 36 sts.
P 1 row.
Working in st st (1 row k, 1 row p), inc 1 st at each end of next 7 rows. 50 sts.
P 1 row.
Inc 1 st at each end of next and every foll alt row to 60 sts.
Cont in st st until bag measures 5½in (14cm) from beg, ending with a p row.

Shape top and strap
Next Row K19, k2tog and turn.
Working on these 20 sts only, dec 1 st at beg of next and at the same edge of next 5 rows. 14 sts.
P 1 row.
**Dec 1 st at shaped edge on next and every foll alt row to 9 sts.
Cont in st st without shaping until strap measures 3½in (9cm) from last dec, ending with a p row.
Buttonhole Row 1 K3, bind off 3 sts, k to end.
Buttonhole Row 2 P3, cast on 3 sts, p to end.
Cont in st st until strap measures 5in (12.5cm) from last dec, ending with a p row.
Bind off.**
With RS of work facing, slip 18 sts onto a stitch holder, rejoin yarn, ssk, k to end. 20 sts.
Dec 1 st at end of next and at the same edge of next 5 rows. 14 sts.
P 1 row.
Work as given for first strap from ** to **.

Large pocket
Using size 3 (3.25mm) needles, cast on 35 sts.
K 4 rows.
Work in st st, starting with a p row, until pocket measures 3in (7.5cm) from beg, ending with a p row.

Shape corners
Bind off 5 sts at beg of next 2 rows. 25 sts.
Work ¾in (2cm) in st st, ending with a p row.
Bind off.

Flap
Using size 3 (3.25mm) needles, cast on 25 sts.
K 4 rows.
Next Row K3, p19, k3.
Buttonhole Row 1 K4, bind off 3 sts, k to last 7 sts, bind off 3 sts, k to end.
Buttonhole Row 2 K3, p1, cast on 3 sts, p11, cast on 3 sts, p1, k3.
Next Row K to end.
Next Row K3, p19, k3.
Rep the last 2 rows until flap measures 2¼in (5.5cm) from beg, ending with a p row.
Bind off.

Phone pocket
Using size 3 (3.25mm) needles, cast on 25 sts.
K 4 rows.
Work in st st, starting with a p row, until pocket measures 4in (10cm) from beg, ending with a p row.

Shape corners

Bind off 5 sts at beg of next 2 rows. 15 sts.
Work ¾in (2cm) in st st, ending with a p row.
Bind off.

Flap

Using size 3 (3.25mm) needles, cast on 15 sts.
K 4 rows.
Next Row K3, p9, k3.
Buttonhole Row 1 K6, bind off 3 sts, k to end.
Buttonhole Row 2 K3, p3, cast on 3 sts, p3, k3.
Next Row K to end.
Next Row K3, p9, k3.
Rep the last 2 rows until flap measures 2¼in
(5.5cm) from beg, ending with a p row.
Bind off.

to finish...

Sew in all ends neatly – the finished edges will
show on the outside of the bag. Press according to
instructions on ball band.

Zip edging

With RS of back facing, using size 3 (3.25mm)
needles and beg at last dec, pick up and knit 17
sts down right strap shaping, slip 18 sts from stitch
holder onto a needle and k18, pick up and knit 17
sts up left strap shaping to last dec. 52 sts.
Bind off knitwise.
Work zip edging on front the same.

Sew the corners of the pockets closed by placing
the short side seam to the bound-off sts with WS
together. Sew together using a neat flat running
stitch. To position the pockets, lay the front down
flat. Place markers 10 sts in from each side seam.
Count 15 sts in from left-hand marker and place
a marker. Count 5 rows up from base and place a
marker. Place WS of phone pocket onto RS of front,
matching the left-side edge to the column of sts
marked by left-hand marker and the pocket base to
row of sts marked by base marker. Using flat running
stitch, sew the left side of the phone pocket from
base to top edge. Sew base of pocket along row
of stitches marked by base marker. Sew right-side
edge up column of sts marked by centre marker. Do
not flatten the pocket or sew it flat – it should stand
away from the front. Place WS of large pocket onto
RS of front, matching left side to edge of phone
pocket and top to top edge of phone pocket. Using

flat running stitch, sew large pocket into position.
Remove markers. Place each flap above its pocket
with RS to RS of front. Sew base of each flap 2 rows
above top edge of pockets. With WS facing, place
back and front together. Using flat running stitch,
sew outside seam from top of right strap around
edge to top of left strap. Sew together top of each
strap. Sew from top of strap down to beg of zip
edging on each side. Sew around buttonholes to
join front to back to make one buttonhole. Sew in
zip (see page 117). Fold flaps over pockets and
mark positions of buttons. Sew on buttons. With
front facing, sew a button onto the RS of right strap
1in (2.5cm) above buttonhole. Sew a button onto
the WS of left strap 1in (2.5cm) above buttonhole.
On the front, sew a button in centre of each strap
in line with beg of zip edging. Place straps around
belt and button each strap down to front.

hands-free handbag

MEASUREMENTS
Finished bag measures 9½in (24cm) wide
and 5½in (14cm) high from base to zip

GATHER TOGETHER...
Materials
3 x 1¾oz (50g) balls of light-weight (DK)
alpaca/silk-mix yarn (114yd/105m per ball)
in pink

Needles and notions
1 pair of size 3 (3.25mm) needles
Stitch holder
Stitch markers
8in (20.5cm)-long zip
7 ¾in (2cm) diameter buttons

GAUGE
26 sts and 37 rows to 4in (10cm) measured
over st st using size 3 (3.25mm) needles

YARN FOCUS
I wanted a contrast to the smart, sharp khaki yarn
of the belt bag. The angora in this yarn adds a
fuzzy appearance, while the silk makes it fluid
and soft. Hot pink is gorgeous and feminine, but
also funky and wild.

Here, we show how the belt bag can be converted into a handbag, and is
easy to change back again. Made in a less structured yarn, and a fabulous
sassy hot pink colour, this is a softer look for a utilitarian bag.

DESIGN SECRETS UNRAVELLED...
This bag would look great in a robust tweed wool
to go with thick winter sweaters and scarves. For
summer, you could use cotton or linen in pastel
shades. Add handmade or painted wooden buttons
for a special touch.

Knit your bag...
Work exactly as given for Look, No Hands!
bag. Place ends of straps over each other
and button together.

bowled over

This bowling bag is a classic, versatile shape. This version, in denim yarn, combines a casual feel with a sophisticated, stylish shape. The bag is large enough, and sturdy enough, to be useful as an everyday bag, but, if knitted in other yarns and colourways, would work equally well as a more dressy bag for special occasions. The butterfly motif adds a touch of colour and glamour, and stands out smartly against the dense texture of the bag.

The appliquéd butterfly motif adds a stylish detail to this chic bag; the colours tone in pleasingly together.

DESIGN SECRETS UNRAVELLED...

You could make this bag in virtually any medium-weight (aran) yarn. Pick a yarn that has some body to it; this bag relies on being able to hold its shape. It wouldn't be suitable for a light yarn such as mohair or silk. It would, however, look very smart in a wool yarn in deep brown with cream handles. Or you could make it funky with two contrasting bright-coloured cottons such as pink and orange. Add a patch with your initials or a cluster of buttons and beads.

YARN FOCUS

Bowling bags are robust, everyday bags and I have chosen a denim yarn to reflect this. This is 100% cotton in an aged denim blue. I wanted contrasting handles, so chose a mercerized cotton in dark blue.

bowled over

MEASUREMENTS

Finished bag measures 12in (30.5cm)
wide at base and 8in (20.5cm) high and
4in (10cm) deep

GATHER TOGETHER...
Materials

A 4 x 1¾oz (50g) balls of medium-weight (aran)
cotton yarn (74yd/68m per ball) in denim blue
B 1 x 1¾oz (50g) ball of light-weight (DK)
mercerized cotton yarn (115yd/106m per ball)
in navy

Needles and notions

1 pair of size 7 (4.5mm) needles
2 size 3 (3.25mm) double-pointed needles
Stitch markers
2 8in (20.5cm) jeans zips
Lining fabric 30in (76cm) x 35in (89cm)
Heavyweight sew-in interfacing
20in (51cm) x 14in (35.5cm)
28in (71cm) of ¼in (0.6cm) thick piping
cord for handles
Thick card for base
Appliqué patch

GAUGE

19 sts and 30 rows to 4in (10cm) measured
over seed (UK: moss) st using size 7
(4.5mm) needles

This bag is worked in seed (UK: moss) stitch for a thick textured fabric. The only shaping occurs on the front and back; the rest of the pieces are unshaped. Two jeans zips are used to fasten the bag and the contrasting handles are strengthened with piping cord. The sides are stiffened with heavyweight interfacing, which helps the bag keep its upright shape. The base is strengthened with a removable insert of thick card. An appliqué patch adds a pleasing finishing touch.

knit your bag...

Back and Front (make 2 the same)
Using size 7 (4.5mm) needles and A, cast
on 57 sts.
Row 1 RS K1, *p1, k1; rep from * to end.
This row forms seed (UK: moss) st. Work a further
21 rows in seed (UK moss) st.

Shape sides

Keeping seed (UK: moss) st correct, dec 1 st at
each end of next and foll 8th. 53 sts.
Patt 5 rows. Place a marker at each end of last row.
Dec 1 st at each end of next and foll 4th row.
49 sts.
Patt 1 row.
Dec 1 st at each end of next and every foll alt row
to 39 sts.
Dec 1 st at each end of foll 3 rows. 33 sts.
Bind off in patt 4 sts at beg of next 2 rows. 25 sts.
Bind off in patt 5 sts at beg of next 2 rows. 15 sts.
Bind off in patt rem sts.

Base

Using size 7 (4.5mm) needles and A, cast on
19 sts.
Work in seed (UK: moss) st until base measures
12in (30.5cm) from beg.
Bind off in patt.

Side panel (make 2)
Using size 7 (4.5mm) needles and A, cast
on 19 sts.
Work 36 rows in seed (UK: moss) st.
Bind off in patt.

Zip panel (make 2)
Using size 7 (4.5mm) needles and A, cast on 8 sts.
Row 1 RS *K1, p1; rep from * to end.
Row 2 *P1, k1; rep from * to end.
Rep these 2 rows until zip panel fits around top of
front from marker to marker.
Bind off.

Handles
Flat end
Using size 3 (3.25mm) double-pointed needles
and B, cast on 9 sts and, working back and forth in
flat knitting, work 8 rows in st st (1 row k, 1 row p),
starting with a k row.
Dec 1 st at each end of next and foll alt row. 5 sts.
Purl 1 row.

Knitted cord
(See page 121 for more on knitting cord.) Knit 1
row. Do not turn the work but slide the sts to the
other end of the needle. Pull up the yarn and knit
the sts again. Repeat until handle measures 14in
(35.5cm) from cast-on edge.

Flat end
Resuming working back and forth, purl 1 row.
Working in st st, inc 1 st at each end of next
and foll alt row. 9 sts.
Work 8 rows in st st.
Bind off.

to finish...
Sew in all ends. Press according to instructions
on ball band.

Lining
Make a stiffened lining as shown on page 116.
Sew the zip into the zip panels.

Base
Cut a piece of greyboard 12in (30.5cm) long and
4in (10cm) wide. Make a base as shown on page
116. Cut 2 pieces of piping cord 14in (35.5cm)
long. Thread each piece through a handle, making
sure the ends of the cord are covered by the flat
ends. Mark the position of the handles on the front
by measuring 4in (10cm) down from the top in the
centre. Place a pin. Using this as the centre, place

a pin 1¾in (4.5cm) each side. These pins mark
the edge of the flat end of the handle. Sew on the
handle, working a few stitches through the piping
cord to secure it. Repeat for the other handle on
the back. Sew on the appliqué patch between the
handles. Sew the base and side panels to the front.
Sew the back onto the base and side panels. Join
the corner seams. Sew the zip panel around the
top of the back and front.

With WS together, slip the lining into the bag. To
hold the lining in position, sew the corner seams
of the lining and the bag together and sew the
seam between the side and zip panels on the bag
and lining together. Slipstitch the knitted zip panels
to the zip close to the zip teeth. Push base into bag
so that it lies flat.

when the cows come home

A lot of the projects in this book are chic, classy and sophisticated. This bag lets out your fun, silly side – after all, we don't have to be grown up all the time. This exuberant cow-print shoulder bag is roomy enough for shopping, carrying your latest knitting project or packing for a weekend break – and it will certainly turn heads, whether you're in the city or the country!

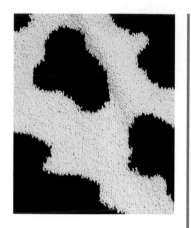

Here, the astrakhan yarn adds a pleasing texture and tactility to this innovative bag.

DESIGN SECRETS UNRAVELLED...

You might prefer to use brown instead of black – or you could be even more outrageous and change the colours entirely. Go for two funky colours together, such as purple and lime green, or yellow and orange, or go for pale shades of blue or green. You could work the patches in a longer-pile yarn like an eyelash or thick chenille and contrast it with a smooth yarn for the background. Be as creative as you like.

YARN FOCUS

I wanted a short texture for this cow-print pattern. I considered using a short-pile eyelash yarn or a chenille, but instead opted for this bubbly astrakhan-effect yarn. For intarsia (the technique used to work the colour changes in the pattern – see pages 108–109), you need yarns that will lie nicely against each other, not slipping when twisted together or being difficult to pull up tightly to close any holes when changing colour.

when the cows come home

MEASUREMENTS
Finished bag measures 16in (40.5cm) wide and
14in (35.5cm) high and 4in (10cm) deep at base

GATHER TOGETHER...
Materials
3 x 1¾oz (50g) balls of medium-weight (aran)
astrakhan or bouclé yarn (76yd/70m per ball)
in each of white (**A**) and black (**B**)
Oddments of light-weight (DK) yarn in black
and white for sewing up

Needles and notions
1 pair of size 7 (4.5mm) needles
Lining fabric 36in (91.5cm) x 20in (51cm)
Thick card for base
52in (132cm) length of 1in (2.5cm) wide
webbing or petersham ribbon for handles

GAUGE
18 sts and 25 rows to 4in (10cm) measured
over st st using size 7 (4.5mm) needles

The large blocks of colour for this pattern are simply knitted using the intarsia technique (see pages 108–109). The chart is easy to work from; the back and front are both the same. The handles are made from strong webbing tape and the bag is lined with hard-wearing calico. The flat base is strengthened with a removable insert of thick card.

Knit your bag...
Front and Back (make 2 the same)
Using size 7 (4.5mm) needles and A, cast
on 54 sts.
Row 1 RS K13A, k41B.
Row 2 P41B, p13A.
Rep these 2 rows 5 times more.
Keeping colours correct, cast on 9 sts at beg
of next 2 rows. 72 sts.
Commence chart.
Reading RS (odd) rows from right to left and WS
(even) rows from left to right, work in st st until
row 85 has been completed.
Turning Row WS K17B, k21A, k34B.
Next Row K34B, k21A, k17B.
Next Row P17B, p21A, p34B.
Rep the last 2 rows twice more.
Bind off.

to finish...
Sew in all ends. Press according to instructions
on ball band.

Lining
Make a lining with a flat base as shown on pages
115–116. Cut webbing into two lengths for handles
and sew securely onto the wrong side of the lining.

Base
Cut a piece of thick card 13in (18cm) long and 4in
(5cm) wide. Make a base as shown on page 116.
Join base and side seams. Place side seam along
base seam and join corner seams. Fold facing
over and slipstitch into position. Insert lining and
slipstitch to facing. Sew through handles to secure
to knitted pieces.

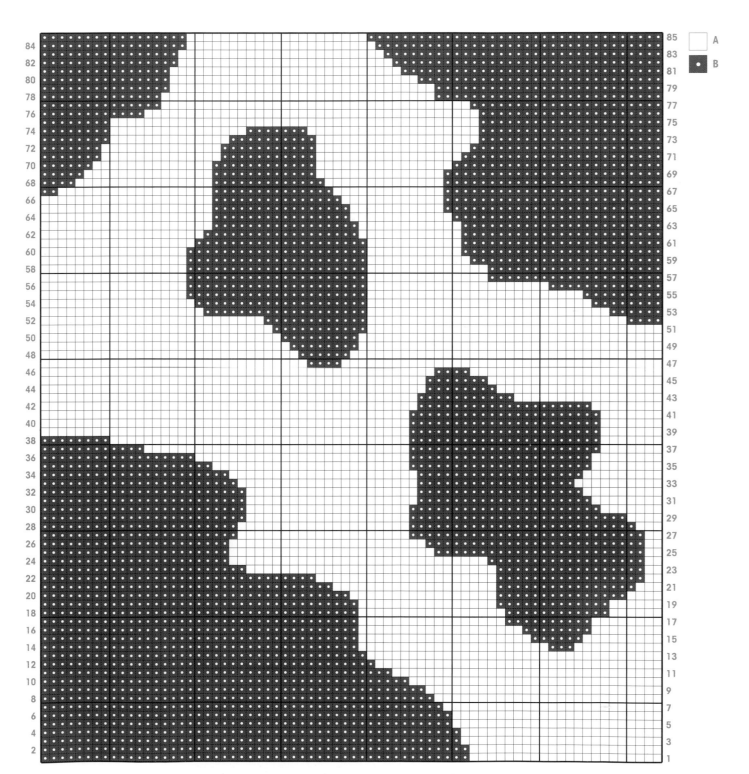

frills and flounces

If you ever feel the need to get in touch with your feminine side, then this is the bag for you – it's gloriously frivolous; frilly, frothy, fun and funky. It's just the thing to add a colourful and whimsical touch to an outfit. The bag also has some body and substance, so it will keep its shape; it's not purely decorative. And there is still plenty of room inside for you to fit in all the essentials you need to carry around with you.

DESIGN SECRETS UNRAVELLED…

You could use a contrasting textured yarn for the frills. How about metallic on a matte background, or a smooth ribbon against a background of tweed wool? Choose contrasting colours such as a hot pink with fiery orange frills, or dark purple with funky lime green. Or choose colours that are closer to each other; sea green with blue, or camel with chocolate brown.

YARN FOCUS

I wanted the frills to stick out and retain their form during use, so I chose this light-weight (DK) cotton yarn. It has body and a heaviness that means the frills won't be crushed; nor will the bag lose its shape. Attention is fully on the bright red frills, while the background is in a complementary shade of plum.

frills and spills

MEASUREMENTS
Finished bag measures 9in (23cm) wide and 8in
(20.5cm) high and 2in (5cm) deep at base

GATHER TOGETHER...
Materials
A 2 x 1¾oz (50g) balls of light-weight (DK)
cotton-mix yarn (98yd/90m per ball) in plum
B 2 x 1¾oz (50g) balls of light-weight (DK)
cotton yarn (93yd/85m per ball) in red

Needles and notions
2 pairs of size 6 (4mm) needles
Lining fabric 22in (56cm) x 20in (51cm)
Thick card for base

GAUGE
20 sts and 28 rows to 4in (10cm) measured over
st st using size 6 (4mm) needles and yarn A

The frills on this bag are worked first. There are a lot of stitches to cast on, but these are immediately decreased by half and then by half again. Keep these frills on separate needles, ready for knitting into the stockinette-stitch background. The corners are shaped to give a flat base, which is strengthened with a removable insert of thick card.

Knit your bag...
Frills (make 8)
Using size 6 (4mm) needles and B, cast on 180 sts.
Row 1 *K2, lift first of these 2 sts over second and off the needle: rep from * to end. 90 sts.
Row 2 *P2tog: rep from * to end. 45 sts.
Leave these sts on a spare needle.

Front
Using size 6 (4mm) needles and A, cast on 35 sts.
Work 6 rows in st st (1 row k, 1 row p) starting with a k row.
Cast on 5 sts at beg of next 2 rows. 45 sts.**
Work 4 rows in st st.
***Join in frill
Place needle holding frill in front of left-hand needle with RS facing out. Insert the right-hand needle through first st of frill then through first st of bag. Using A, draw a loop through both sts, knitting them together. Slip both sts off their needles. Repeat for each set of two sts to end of row.
Using A, work 7 rows in st st.
Rep from *** 5 times more.
Using B, join in 7th frill.

Facing
****Using B, work 3 rows in st st, starting with a k row.
Work 4 rows in st st, starting with a k row.
Bind off.

Back
Work as given for Front to **.
Work 3 rows in st st.
*** Using B, work 1 row.
Using A, work 7 rows.

Rep from *** 5 times more.
Using A, purl 1 row.
Using B, join in frill.
Work facing as given for Front from ****.

Handles (make 2)
Using size 6 (4mm) needles and A, cast on 60 sts.
Using A, work 6 rows in st st, starting with a k row.
Using B, work 6 rows in st st.
Using B, bind off.

to finish...
Sew in all ends. Press according to instructions on ball band.

Lining
Make a lining with a flat base (pages 115–116).

Base
Cut a piece of thick card 7in (18cm) long and 2in (5cm) wide. Make a base as shown on page 116. Using B, and starting at the top of the bag, sew the side seams together, joining the facings and the top frill. Using A, join the remainder of the side seams, enclosing the ends of the other frills into the seam. Join the base seam. To form the bottom corners, turn the bag inside out. Place side seam along base seam and join corner seam. Sew other corner to match. Turn through to RS. Fold facing over to WS and slipstitch into position. Fold handles in half and sew cast-on and bound-off edges together. Sew handles into place, 2½in (6cm) from side seams. With WS together, slip the lining into the bag and slipstitch neatly into place onto the facing, covering the ends of the handles. Push base into bag so that it lies flat.

MEASUREMENTS

Finished bag measures 8½in (21.5cm) wide and 7½in (19cm) high and 2in (5cm) deep at base

GATHER TOGETHER...

Materials

2 x 1¾oz (50g) balls of light-weight (DK) alpaca/wool-mix tweed yarn (197yd/180m per ball) in pink

Needles and notions

2 pairs of size 6 (4mm) needles
Lining fabric 22in (56cm) x 20in (51cm)
Thick card for base

GAUGE

21sts and 29 rows to 4in (10cm) measured over st st using size 6 (4mm) needles

YARN FOCUS

I chose a fantastic alpaca/wool-mix yarn for this version of the frilly bag. The colour too is mixed – light pink with a twist of dark pink. By working in a softer yarn, the bag becomes airy. In one colour, the frills merge into the bag to create a three-dimensional fabric, rather than standing stiffly apart from it.

This one-colour version of the bag is just as frilly but lighter and even more feminine. It is worked in exactly the same way, but uses only one colour in a softer yarn.

Knit your bag...

Frills, Front and Back

Work as given for Frills and Spills, using one colour throughout.

Handles (make 2)

Using size 6 (4mm) needles, cast on 60 sts.
Work 6 rows in st st, starting with a k row.
Bind off.

to finish...

Sew in all ends. Press according to instructions on ball band. Do not press handles, allow them to roll.

Lining, Base and Making Up

Work as given for Frills and Spills.

DESIGN SECRETS UNRAVELLED...

This is a delicate shade of pink, but using a hot pink instead would create a funkier look. Use an earthy shade of wool tweed for a surprising winter bag. A ribbon yarn would make the frills and the whole bag more fluid, while a metallic yarn would make it crisp and bold.

square dance

This bag is worked in mitred squares. Although it looks like patches sewn together, there is very little sewing involved. The stunning colour effects are achieved by using a multi-coloured yarn rather than different yarns of individual colours. Mitred squares create a stunning geometric effect that is truly eye-catching. The bag can be either be fulled, as this one was, or left as knitted. Fulling will give it a dense, felt-like texture that is very attractive, while leaving the bag unfulled allows the colours to stand out clearly.

Knitting mitred squares in a multi-coloured yarn creates a beautiful bag full of interesting shapes and wonderful colour effects.

YARN FOCUS

The technique of knitting mitred squares is shown off best in a multi-coloured or self-striping yarn. This yarn runs from light turquoise through pink and mauve to yellow and orange. I cut out a few colours that I didn't like, but basically I used the yarn continuously, going with the colour sequence into the next square. Because I wanted to full this bag, I needed to use a 100% wool yarn.

DESIGN SECRETS UNRAVELLED...

If you don't want to full this bag, you can work with any fibre; you don't need to keep to wool. The seed (UK: moss) stitch would look great in a crisp cotton, or a wool would blend the stitches together. To have more control over the choice of colours and to introduce other textures, you could make up your own multi-yarn ball. First, gather a collection of yarns and colours together. Pull out two arm's lengths of the first yarn and wind it into a ball. Tie on the second colour, leaving long ends to weave in during knitting. Pull out three arm's lengths and continue winding onto the ball. Join on the third colour and pull out one arm's lengths and wind it onto the ball. Continue in this way, changing the colour sequence and the amount of each yarn used each time. Make up a 1¾oz (50g) ball. Knit with this, weaving in the ends as you go.

square dance

The stitches for each piece of this bag are a mixture of casting on or picking up stitches from pieces around it. Detailed instructions are given for working the back and front, which are the same. The squares are worked in seed (UK: moss) stitch, which gives the fabric extra texture. The side gussets and base are then knitted onto the front. The handles consist of a tube with piping cord threaded through for extra strength.

Knit your bag...
Back and Front (make 2)
L Shape 1 (LS1)

Using size 8 (5mm) needles, cast on 51 sts.
Row 1 WS K1, (p1, k1) 3 times, p3tog, (k1, p1) 7 times, k3tog, (p1, k1) 7 times, p3tog, (k1, p1) 3 times, sl1 wyif. 45 sts.
Row 2 and every foll RS row *K1, p1; rep from * to last st, sl1 wyif.
Row 3 (k1, p1) 3 times, k3tog, (p1, k1) 6 times, p3tog, (k1, p1) 6 times, k3tog, (p1, k1) twice, p1, sl1 wyif. 39 sts.
Row 5 K1, (p1, k1) twice, p3tog, (k1, p1) 5 times, k3tog, (p1, k1) 5 times, p3tog, (k1, p1) twice, sl1 wyif. 33 sts.
Row 7 (K1, p1) twice, k3tog, (p1, k1) 4 times, p3tog, (k1, p1) 4 times, k3tog, p1, k1, p1, sl1 wyif. 27 sts.
Row 9 K1, p1, k1, p3tog, (k1, p1) 3 times, k3tog, (p1, k1) 3 times, p3tog, k1, p1, sl1 wyif. 21 sts.
Row 11 K1, p1, k3tog, (p1, k1) twice, p3tog, (k1, p1) twice, k3tog, p1, sl1 wyif. 15 sts.
Row 13 K1, p3tog, k1, p1, k3tog, p1, k1, p3tog, sl1 wyif. 9 sts.
Row 15 K3tog tbl, p3tog, k3tog. 3 sts.
Row 16 K3tog. 1 st.
Cut yarn and thread through rem st.

Square 2 (S2)
Cast on 8 sts, with RS of LS1 facing, pick up and knit 9 sts along right short edge. 17 sts.
Row 1 WS K1, (p1, k1) 3 times, p3tog, (k1, p1) 3 times, sl1 wyif. 15 sts.
Row 2 and every foll RS row *K1, p1; rep from * to last st, sl1 wyif.
Row 3 (K1, p1) 3 times, k3tog, (p1, k1) twice, p1, sl1 wyif. 13 sts.
Row 5 K1, (p1, k1) twice, p3tog, (k1, p1) twice, sl1 wyif. 11 sts.
Row 7 (K1, p1) twice, k3tog, p1, k1, p1, sl1 wyif. 9 sts.
Row 9 K1, p1, k1, p3tog, k1, p1, sl1 wyif. 7 sts.
Row 11 K1, p1, k3tog, p1, sl1 wyif. 5 sts.
Row 13 K1, p3tog, sl1 wyif. 3 sts.
Row 15 K3tog tbl. 1 st.
Cut yarn and thread through rem st.

L Shape 3 (LS3)
Cast on 8 sts, pick up and knit 9 sts along top of S2, 17 sts around inside edge of LS1, cast on 17 sts. 51 sts.
Work L shape as given for LS1.

Square 4 (S4)
Pick up and knit 9 sts along edge of LS3 and 8 sts along edge of LS1. 17 sts.
Work square as given for S2.

L Shape 5 (LS5)
Cast on 8 sts, pick up and knit 9 sts along edge of LS3, 9 sts along edge of S4, cast on 25 sts. 51 sts.
Work L shape as given for LS1.

L Shape 6 (LS6)
Cast on 17 sts, pick up and knit 17 sts around inside edge of LS3, 9 sts along edge of LS5, cast on 8 sts. 51 sts.
Work L shape as for LS1.

Rectangle 7 (R7)
Cast on 8 sts, pick up and knit 9 sts along edge of LS6, and 17 sts around inside edge of LS5. 34 sts.

Row 1 WS K1, (p1, k1) 3 times, p3tog, (k1, p1) 7 times, k3tog, (p1, k1) 3 times, sl1 wyif. 30 sts.
Row 2 and every foll RS row K2, p1, * k1, p1; rep from * to last st, sl1 wyif.
Row 3 (k1, p1) 3 times, k3tog, (p1, k1) 6 times, p3tog, (k1, p1) twice, sl1 wyif. 26 sts.
Row 5 K1, (p1, k1) twice, p3tog, (k1, p1) 5 times, k3tog, (p1, k1) twice, sl1 wyif. 22 sts.
Row 7 (K1, p1) twice, k3tog, (p1, k1) 4 times, p3tog, k1, p1, k1, sl1 wyif. 18 sts.
Row 9 K1, p1, k1, p3tog, (k1, p1) 3 times, k3tog, p1, k1, sl1 wyif. 14 sts.
Row 11 K1, p1, k3tog, (p1, k1) twice, p3tog, k1, sl1 wyif. 10 sts.
Row 13 K1, p3tog, k1, p1, k3tog, sl1 wyif. 6 sts.
Row 15 K3tog tbl, p3tog. 2 sts.
Row 16 K2tog. 1 st.
Cut yarn and thread through rem st.

L Square 8 (LS8)
Pick up and knit 17 sts around inside edge of LS6, 9 sts along edge of R7, cast on 25 sts. 51 sts.
Work L shape as given for LS1.

Rectangle 9 (R9)
Cast on 8 sts, pick up and knit 9 sts along edge of LS6, and 17 sts around inside edge of LS8. 34 sts.
Work rectangle as given for R7.

L Shape 10 (LS10)
Cast on 8 sts, pick up and knit 9 sts along edge of S2, 9 sts along edge of LS3, 8 sts along edge of LS6, 9 sts along edge of R9, cast on 8 sts. 51 sts.
Work L shape as given LS1.

Square 11 (S11)
Pick up and knit 17 sts around inside of LS10. 17 sts.
Work square as given for S2.

Side gussets and base
Rectangle 12 (R12)
Cast on 8 sts, with RS of Front facing, pick up and knit 18 sts along edge of LS5, cast on 8 sts. 34 sts.
Work rectangle as given for R7.

Square 13 (S13)
Pick up and knit 9 sts along edge of R12, and 8 sts along edge of S4. 17 sts.
Work square as given for S2.

Rectangle 14 (R14)
Pick up and knit 9 sts along S13, 17 sts along edge of LS1, cast on 8 sts. 34 sts.

Work rectangle as given for R7.

Rectangle 15 (R15)
Pick up and knit 8 sts along edge of R14, 18 sts along edge of LS1, cast on 8 sts. 34 sts.
Work rectangle as given for R7.

Square 16 (S16)
Pick up and knit 8 sts along edge of R15, and 9 sts along edge of S2. 17 sts.
Work square as given for S2.

Rectangle 17 (R17)
Pick up and knit 8 sts along edge of S16, 9 sts along edge of LS10, 9 sts along edge of S11, cast on 8 sts. 34 sts.
Work rectangle as given for R7.

Rectangle 18 (R18)
Pick up and knit 8 sts along edge of R17, 9 sts along edge of S11, 9 sts along edge of LS10, cast on 8 sts. 34 sts.
Work rectangle as given for R7.

Square 19 (S19)
Pick up and knit 8 sts along edge of R18, 9 sts along edge to centre of R9. 17 sts.
Work square as given for S2.

Rectangle 20 (R20)
Pick up and knit 8 sts along edge of S19, 8 sts along edge of R9, 9 sts along edge of LS8, cast on 8 sts. 34 sts.
Work rectangle as given for R7.

Facing
Join back to front and gussets by joining left side seam. Using size 8 (5mm) needles and with RS of work facing, pick up and knit 9 sts across top edge of side gusset, 43 sts across front, 9 sts across side gusset and 43 sts across back. 104 sts.
Work 3 rows in rev st st, starting with a k row.
Work 3 rows in st st, starting with a k row.
Bind off loosely.

Handles (make 2)
Flat end
Using size 6 (4mm) double-pointed needles, cast on 9 sts and, working back and forth in flat knitting, work 8 rows in st st, starting with a k row.
Dec 1 st at each end of next and foll alt row. 5 sts.
Purl 1 row.

Knitted tubular cord
Knit 1 row. Do not turn the work but slide the sts to the other end of the needle. Pull up the yarn and knit the sts again. Repeat until handle measures 23in (57cm) from cast-on edge. (See page 121 for more on knitting cord.)

Flat end
Resuming working back and forth, purl 1 row.
Working in st st, inc 1 st at each end of next and foll alt row. 9 sts.
Work 8 rows in st st.
Bind off.

to finish...
Sew in all ends. Press according to instructions on ball band. Join remaining side seam and base seam. Fold facing to the WS and slipstitch into position. Cut two pieces of piping cord 23in (57cm) long. Bind the ends with sewing thread to prevent them unravelling. Thread a piece of piping cord through each of the handles. Use the crochet hook to knit up the ladder on the handles (see page 122). Sew the handles into position, 2in (5cm) from side seams and 2½in (6cm) from top edge, working stitches through the piping cord to secure. Full the bag according to the instructions on page 111.

Lining and base
Make a lining and base as shown on pages 115–116. With WS together, slip the lining into the bag and slipstitch neatly into place onto the facing. Push base into bag so that it lies flat.

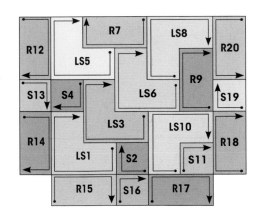

quick draw

Downsize your clutter into this drawstring bag and wear it on your wrist. The daintiness of this bag offers a welcome alternative for occasions when you don't want to lug around your usual backpack, shoulder bag or tote. The subtly furry texture and the silky tassel add an extra element of elegance and glamour. The small size of this bag makes it an ideal item to experiment with new yarns – you won't need much to tell whether or not you like the effect. It would also be a good way to use up any yarn left over from making a special garment.

The eyelash yarns used in this bag create a subtle hazy, gauzy effect that is wonderfully tactile.

DESIGN SECRETS UNRAVELLED...

You could make a version of this bag in light summer shades or in a rich colour for evening. Choose your favourite colour; it could be rich purple, hot pink, sea green, or sunny yellow. Collect it in four contrasting textures of light-weight (DK) yarn; slub, eyelash, smooth wool, bouclé, ribbon, or shiny viscose. Add a ready-made tassel or make up your own and tie on beads, buttons or shells for a special finishing touch.

YARN FOCUS

Using a limited colour palette meant that I could concentrate on texture; here I used a long shimmering eyelash yarn next to a matte soft cotton, and a bubbly slub yarn with a crisp silky crepe. Each yarn holds the colour differently and together they create a fantastic snow-inspired bag.

snow queen

MEASUREMENTS

5in (12.5cm) wide and 7in (18cm) long
(excluding tassel)

GATHER TOGETHER...
Materials

A 1 x 1¾oz (50g) ball of light-weight (DK)
fake-fur yarn (98yd/90m per ball) in white

B 1 x 1¾oz (50g) ball of light-weight (DK)
cotton (104yd/95m per ball) in white

C 1 x 1¾oz (50g) ball of light-weight (DK)
slub-textured yarn (140yd/128m per ball) in white

D 1 x 1¾oz (50g) ball of light-weight (DK)
crepe yarn (147yd/135m per ball) in white

Needles and notions

1 pair of size 6 (4mm) needles
14in (35.5cm) length of cord
Tassel

GAUGE

22 sts and 28 rows to 4in (10cm) measured
over st st (1 row k, 1 row p) using size 6 (4mm)
needles and B

Worked in simple stockinette stitch, this drawstring bag is like a winter wedding; icy, crisp and elegant. Each stripe is in a different yarn of only one colour. A cord is threaded through a row of eyelets, made with a yo and k2tog. The base is shaped to a point using ssk (see pages 105–107 for these increasing and decreasing techniques). Attach a ready-made tassel or make your own (see page 121).

Knit your bag...

Using size 6 (4mm) needles and A, cast on 58 sts
and knit 4 rows.
Using B, p 1 row.
Eyelet Row RS Using B, k4, (yo, k2tog, k5) 7 times,
yo, k2tog, k3.
Using B, cont in st st, starting with a p row until
stripe of B measures 2in (5cm) from beg, ending
with a p row.
Using A, k 4 rows.
Using C, work 2in (5cm) in st st, ending with
a p row.
Using A, k 4 rows.

Shape base

Using D throughout, cont as follows:
**Row 1 K1, (ssk, k5) 7 times, ssk, k6. 50 sts.
Row 2 and every foll WS row P.
Row 3 K1, (ssk, k4) 7 times, ssk, k5. 42 sts.
Row 5 K1, (ssk, k3) 7 times, ssk, k4. 34 sts.
Row 7 K1, (ssk, k2) 7 times, ssk, k3. 26 sts.
Row 9 K1, (ssk, k1) 7 times, ssk, k2. 18 sts.
Row 11 K1, (ssk) 8 times, k1. 10 sts.
P 1 row.
Cut yarn, thread through rem sts and pull up tight.

to finish...

Sew in all ends. Press according to instructions on
ball bands. Join side seam. Thread cord through
eyelets and knot ends together. Sew tassel to point
at base.

These bags are a delight to make and give you the scope to explore a colour palette. Why not knit one for each season, and make up a tassel to match?

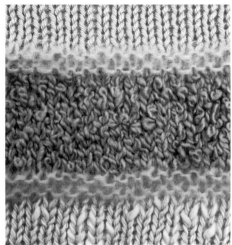

Springtime shimmer

Look to the colours of spring for inspiration. Here I've used four textured yarns in fresh yellow-green with hints of white. All light-weight (DK) yarns, they are a shimmering fake-fur, a softly spun wool, a knitted tape with chips of colour, and a smooth yarn textured with a twist of white bouclé.

Summer shades

For this version, I was inspired by full-bloomed roses on a hot summer afternoon and used yarns in a delicate shade of pink. I used a hazy kid mohair to separate a fresh mercerized cotton, a frivolous astrakhan and a soft matte cotton with loosely spun slubs.

Fall Fantastic

This fiery-coloured short eyelash yarn was a real find and inspired the choice of the other yarns. I used a soft alpaca in deep rust red, and, for the remaining two textures, I made a mix of two yarns, a crisp mercerized cotton together with a fluid ladder tape with squares of orange and pink, and a mix of a tweed wool with a crunchy metallic.

Make up a tassel using stranded cotton embroidery floss in a matching colour. Before trimming the tassel, thread a random mix of soft yellow and white seed beads onto several strands around the outside of the tassel together with a flower-shaped button. Tie a small knot in the end to secure the beads, and trim the tassel neatly.

Choose some large beads that reflect your inspiration; these pink twisted glass roses matched the bag perfectly. Make up a tassel using a smooth yarn from the bag and, before trimming, thread the beads onto strands around the outside. Push them up to the top and secure with a small knot.

Each of the different yarns deserved to be seen on its own, so I made a simple tassel using all the textures and shades together. The ladder ribbon and metallic stand out and add shots of colour to the merging shades of rust, bronze and ginger.

heart on your sleeve

Drawstring bags are very simple to make and wonderfully versatile. This more robust version is knitted to the same pattern as the Snow Queen bag, but is thicker and more cosy. A knitted heart applied with large straight stitch makes for an honest, homespun look.

MEASUREMENTS

6in (15cm) wide and 8in (20.5cm) long
(excluding tassel)

GATHER TOGETHER...
Materials

A 1 x 1¾oz (50g) ball of bulky-weight (chunky) textured wool-mix yarn (120yd/110m per ball) in shades of green
B 1 x ⅞oz (25g) ball of light-weight (DK) mohair (104yd/95m per ball) in purple
Oddment of DK yarn for sewing up and twisted cord

Needles

1 pair of size 8 (5mm) needles

GAUGE

16 sts and 26 rows to 4in (10cm) measured over st st (1 row k, 1 row p) using size 8 (5mm) needles and A

YARN FOCUS

This yarn looked good in a ball, but it was hard to imagine how it would look when knitted up. It features thick lengths of shades of green, running from dark olive to khaki to golden-olive, with thinner lengths of black and white between. Knitted up, it creates a wonderful thick, textured fabric that is warm and soft to touch. The slubby texture is ideal for showing off in stockinette stitch.

Knit your bag...

Using size 8 (5mm) needles and A, cast on 58 sts and knit 4 rows.
P 1 row.
Eyelet Row RS K4, (yo, k2tog, k5) 7 times, yo, k2tog, k3.
Cont in st st, starting with a p row until bag measures 6in (15cm) from beg, ending with a p row.

Shape base

Work as given for Snow Queen from **.

Heart

Using size 3 (3.25mm) needles and B, cast on 3 sts and p 1 row.
Next Row Kf&b, k1, kf&b. 5 sts.
Next Row P.
Next Row Kf&b, k to last 2 ss, kf&b, k1.
Rep the last 2 rows to 17 sts.
Cont in st st until heart measures 2in (5cm) from beg, ending with a p row.

Shape top

Next Row Ssk, k6, bind off 1 st, k to last 2 sts, k2tog.
Working on 7 sts only, p 1 row.
*****Next Row** Ssk, k to last 2 sts, k2tog. 5 sts.
P 1 row.
Next Row Ssk, k1, k2tog. 3 sts.
Bind off.
With WS of work facing, rejoin yarn to second set of 7 sts and p 1 row. Work as given for first side from ***.

to finish...

Sew in all ends. Press according to instructions on ball bands. Using light-weight (DK) yarn, sew heart onto bag using large straight stitches. Using light-weight (DK) yarn, join side seam. Make a twisted cord using 2 strands of light-weight (DK) yarn (see page 121). Thread through eyelets and knot ends together. Using A, make a tassel (see page 121) and sew to point at base.

DESIGN SECRETS UNRAVELLED...

Buy a ball of the most intriguing yarn in the shop; the one with slubs and twists, thick and thin, and multi-coloured. This bag could be made up in wool in shades of fall with a bronze heart, or in silk and viscose in rich purples with a gold heart for a funky evening bag. Try it in cotton and linen for summer, or shades of the sea or hot pink. Knit the heart in a contrasting colour and apply beads; sew it on neatly for a more elegant finish.

fantastic flowers

This is a great bag for a hot summer's day. The vivid colours zing against each other, and the sewed-on leaves add a pleasing three-dimensional touch. The stylish flare shape is created by decreasing the sides and bamboo rings are attached for added impact. Knitted in ever-versatile cotton yarn, this bag is robust enough to take on the beach, and smart and sassy enough to take to summer garden parties and barbecues.

The ready-made bamboo rings are quickly and easily attached and give this bag a stylish finish.

DESIGN SECRETS UNRAVELLED...

You could use pastel shades for a cooler look; try a soft blue background with pale pink flowers and light olive leaves. Try using a different colour for each flower; pinks, purples and mauves, or yellows, oranges and reds. Use yarns with a silk content for a touch of luxury or fluid viscose ribbon yarns for shimmer.

YARN FOCUS

Cotton is available in many vibrant colours; I chose a hot pink background to contrast with the zingy orange flowers and the fresh green leaves. I wanted a matte cotton for its characteristic dry, dusty look; mercerized cotton is harder and the bag wouldn't have gathered onto the handles as softly.

fantastic flowers

MEASUREMENTS

13in (33cm) at widest point and 11in (28cm) long (excluding handles)

GATHER TOGETHER...

Materials

A 3 x 1¾oz (50g) balls of light-weight (DK) cotton (93yd/85m per ball) in pink

B 1x 1¾oz (50g) ball of light-weight (DK) cotton (93yd/85m per ball) in orange

C 1 x 1¾oz (50g) ball of light-weight (DK) cotton (93yd/85m per ball) in green

Needles and notions

1 pair of size 6 (4mm) needles

2 bamboo ring handles

GAUGE

20 sts and 28 rows to 4in (10cm) measured over st st (1 row k, 1 row p) using size 6 (4mm) needles and A

The orange flowers of this colourful bag are worked using intarsia (see page 108–109), while the leaves are knitted separately and sewn on. Simple backstitch (see page 120) is used for the stems and centres of the flowers. The sides are decreased to give a roomy flared shape, while ready-made bamboo ring handles make for a quick finish.

Knit your bag...

Front

Using size 6 (4mm) needles and A, cast on 66 sts. Work 2 rows in st st (1 row k, 1 row p) starting with a k row.

Commence chart

Working RS rows (odd) from right to left and WS rows (even) from left to right, and dec 1 st at each end of 13th and every foll 8th row, work in st st from chart until the 64th row has been completed. 52 sts.

Using A, work 20 rows in st st.

Bind off.

Back

Using size 6 (4mm) needles and A, cast on 66 sts. Work in st st, starting with a k row, dec 1 st at each end of 15th and every foll 8th row to 52 sts. Work 23 rows in st st.

Bind off.

Leaves (make 10)

Using size 6 (4mm) needles and C, cast on 3 sts and p 1 row.

Row 1 RS K1, (yo, k1) twice. 5 sts.

Row 2 and every foll WS row P.

Row 3 K2, yo, k1, yo, k2. 7 sts.

Row 5 K3, yo, k1, yo, k3. 9 sts.

Row 7 Ssk, k5, k2tog. 7 sts.

Row 9 Ssk, k3, k2tog. 5 sts.

Row 11 Ssk, k1, k2tog. 3 sts.

Row 13 Sk2po.

Cut yarn, thread through rem st and pull up tightly.

to finish...

Sew in all ends. Press according to instructions on ball bands. On front, sew a pair of leaves next to each flower (use the photograph for reference). Using C and backstitch (see page 120), work a stem between the leaves and flowers and a swirl in the centre of each flower. Join base seam. Join side seams up to penultimate decrease. Pull top edge through one of the handles from front to back and fold over to enclose the handle. Sew turnover neatly in place using a running stitch. Repeat for other handle.

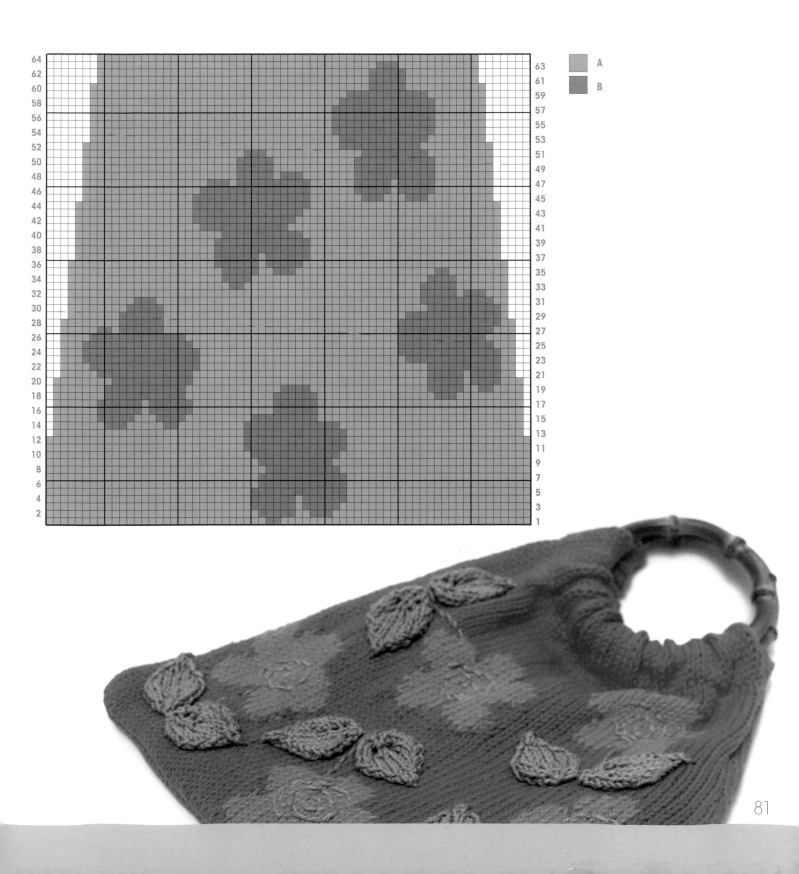

buttons
and bows

This is a wonderfully understated and ladylike bag for occasions when you want to make a sophisticated impression. It is quite a prim bag, reminiscent of smart leather handbags. Its subtle, neutral colour means that it will go with anything in your wardrobe. A simple bow stitch adds a subtle textural interest to the bag's elegant shape, while the single large button adds a neat focal point.

DESIGN SECRETS UNRAVELLED…

This is such a great shape for a bag, it would be a pity to make just one. To create a buttoned-up country-house look, think tweeds and brogues and choose a deep tweed wool with bright flecks of colour. Or think Victorian and choose a deep rich colour such as red or purple and add a jet button. Or for city-slicker chic, try it in smart grey or black with a large leather coat button.

YARN FOCUS

I chose a wonderful soft brown yarn to recreate the look of a leather handbag. This yarn is 100% wool and shows off the neat bow stitch pattern beautifully, pulling the fabric into dimples and waves.

buttons and bows

MEASUREMENTS
Finished bag measures 10½in (26.5cm) wide
and 9in (23cm) high

GATHER TOGETHER...
Materials
3 x 1¾oz (50g) balls of light-weight (DK) wool
(137yd/125m per ball) in light brown

Needles and notions
1 pair of size 5 (3.75mm) needles
2 size 3 (3.25mm) double-pointed needles
Size E (3.5mm) crochet hook
1 large button
17in (43cm) of ¼in (0.6cm)-thick piping cord
for handle

GAUGE
24 sts and 34 rows to 4in (10cm) measured over
texture st using size 5 (3.75mm) needles

SPECIAL ABBREVIATIONS
k-below knit into the next st in the row below
kf&b knit into front and back of st
pf&b purl into front and back of st

The sides of this bag are shaped using kf&b and pf&b (see page 105 for instructions). The flap is shaped into a point with the decreases ssk, k2tog, ssp and p2tog (see page 107). The handle is a tubular cord, with a piping cord threaded through for strength. A large feature button threads through a loop to close the bag.

Knit your bag...
Front and Back (make 2 the same)
Using size 5 (3.75mm) needles, cast on 29 sts.
Row 1 WS P to end.
Row 2 Cast on 6 sts, k to end. 35 sts.
Row 3 Cast on 6 sts, p1, *k3, p3; rep from * to last 4 sts, k3, p1. 41 sts.
Row 4 Cast on 4 sts, k5, *p1, k-below, p1, k3; rep from * to last 4 sts, p1, k-below, p1, k1. 45 sts.
Row 5 Cast on 4 sts, p to end. 49 sts.
Row 6 Kf&b, k to last 2 sts, kf&b, k1.
Row 7 Pf&b, p2, *k3, p3; rep from * to last 6 sts, k3, p1, pf&b, p1. 53 sts.
Row 8 Kf&b, *k3, p1, k-below, p1; rep from * to last 4 sts, k2, kf&b, k1.
Row 9 Pf&b, p to last 2 sts, pf&b, p1. 57 sts.
Row 10 As row 6. 59 sts.
Row 11 P4, *k3, p3; rep from * to last st, p1.
Row 12 As row 8. 61 sts.
Row 13 P to end.
Row 14 As row 6. 63 sts.
Row 15 P3, *k3, p3; rep from * to end.
Row 16 K3, *p1, k-below, p1, k3; rep from * to end.
Row 17 P to end.
Row 18 As row 6. 65 sts.
Row 19 P1, k3, *p3, k3; rep from * to last st, p1.
Row 20 K1, p1, k-below, p1, *k3, p1, k-below, p1; rep from * to last st, k1.
Row 21 P to end.
Row 22 As row 6. 67 sts.
Row 23 P5, *k3, p3; rep from * to last 2 sts, p2.

Row 24 K5, *p1, k-below, p1, k3; rep from * to last 2 sts, k2.
Row 25 P to end.
Row 26 K to end.
Row 27 P2, k3, *p3, k3; rep from * to last 2 sts, p2.
Row 28 K2, p1, k-below, p1, *k3, p1, k-below, p1; rep from * to last 2 sts, k2.
Row 29 P to end.
Row 30 K to end.
Rep rows 23 to 30 once more, then row 23 again.
Row 40 Ssk, k3, *p1, k-below, p1, k3; rep from * to last 2 sts, k2tog.
Keeping texture patt correct, dec 1 st (as set on row 40) at each end of every foll 6th row to 55 sts.
Cont without shaping until work measures approx 9in from beg, ending with a K row.
Turning Row K to end.
Work 4 rows in st st (1 row k, 1 row p) starting with a k row.
Bind off.

Flap (make 2)
Note: keep the edges neat, as these will be seen on the finished bag.
Using size 5 (3.75mm) needles, cast on 55 sts.
Row 1 K to end.
Row 2 P2, k3, *p3, k3; rep from * to last 2 sts, p2.
Row 3 K2, p1, k-below, p1, *k3, p1, k-below, p1; rep from * to last 2 sts, k2.
Row 4 P to end.
Row 5 K to end.

Row 6 P5, *k3, p3; rep from * to last 2 sts, p2.

Row 7 K5, *p1, k-below, p1, k3; rep from * to last 2 sts, k2.

Row 8 P to end.

Rep these 8 rows once more then rows 1 to 4 again.

Next Row Ssk, patt to last 2 sts, k2tog.

Patt 1 row.

Keeping texture patt correct, dec 1 st as set at each end of next and every foll alt row to 45 sts.

Next Row P2tog, patt to last 2 sts, ssp.

Next Row Ssk, patt to last 2 sts, k2tog.

Dec 1 st as set at each end of every row to 35 sts. Bind off 3 sts at beg of next 2 rows, 4 sts at beg of foll 2 rows and 5 sts on foll 2 rows. 11 sts.

Dec 1 st at each end of every row to 3 sts.

Bind off.

Handle
Flat end

Using size 3 (3.25mm) double-pointed needles, cast on 7 sts, and, working back and forth in flat knitting, work 6 rows in st st (1 row k, 1 row p), starting with a k row.

Next Row Ssk, k3, k2tog. 5 sts.

P 1 row.

Knitted tubular cord

Knit 1 row. Do not turn the work but slide the sts to the other end of the needle. Pull up the yarn and knit the sts again. Repeat until handle measures 17in (43cm) from cast-on edge. (See page 121 for more on knitting cord.)

Flat end

Resuming working back and forth, purl 1 row.

Next Row Kf&b, k2, kf&b, k1. 7 sts.

Work 6 rows in st st.

Bind off.

Button loop

Using size 3 (3.25mm) double-pointed needles, cast on 14 sts.

Row 1 K2, bind off 8 sts, k to end.

Row 2 K to end, casting on 8 sts over those bound off in previous row.

Bind off.

to finish...

Sew in all ends. Press according to instructions on ball band. Join back and front. Fold facing at the top to the inside and slipstitch into place. Sew button loop onto point of flap. With WS together, place the flaps together and sew around the edge using a small running stitch. Pin flaps into place on back to cover line of slipstitches from facing. Sew onto back using a small running stitch, through all thicknesses. Cut a piece of piping cord 17in (43cm) long and thread through handle, making sure cord ends are covered by the flat ends. Use the crochet hook to knit up the ladder on the handle (see page 122). Sew the handle into position, next to side seams and below the flaps, working stitches through the piping cord to secure. Fold flap over and mark position of button. Sew on button.

instant messenger

The messenger bag has become the bag of choice for people in a hurry; it is roomy, robust, offers quick access, and is easy and comfortable to wear across the body. This is a style of bag that is strongly associated with modern urban living – motorcycle couriers and so on – but here I've given it a traditional, almost rustic, look, by featuring cable patterns and bobbles that are reminiscent of fishermen's ganseys. The texture is sturdy and resilient.

The cables and bobbles give this bag tremendous textual appeal – they are also satisfying and fun to knit.

DESIGN SECRETS UNRAVELLED...

Cabled fishermen's sweaters are knitted in thick wool, so you could work this bag in a 100% Shetland or handspun wool in a natural colour for a traditional look. Alternatively, give it a modern twist by using a brightly coloured rayon for shine or a velour ribbon for a mock suede fabric. For a smarter look, try a smooth cashmere or silk mix. For eco-warriors, try linen or hemp in earth shades.

YARN FOCUS

The cotton/silk mix that I used for this bag has great texture; it is dry, slightly rough, and it looks worn even when newly knitted. I chose this fantastic blue because it is very like denim. The cables and bobbles really stand out from the background, making a thick fabric.

instant messenger

MEASUREMENTS

Finished bag measures 14in (35.5cm) wide, 11in (28cm) high and 1¾in (4.5cm) deep

GATHER TOGETHER...
Materials

7 x 1¾oz (50g) balls of medium-weight (aran) silk/cotton-mix yarn (118yd/108m per ball) in denim blue

Needles and notions

1 pair of size 7 (4.5mm) needles
Cable needle
Stitch markers
Lining fabric 20in (51cm) x 40in (101.5cm)
85in (216cm) of 1½in (4cm)-wide webbing tape
1 button

GAUGE

19 sts and 25 rows to 4in (10cm) measured over moss st (UK: double moss st) using size 7 (4.5mm) needles

Special Abbreviations

C4F sl 2 sts on to cable needle at front, k2, k2 from cable needle.

C4B sl 2 sts on to cable needle at back, k2, k2 from cable needle.

C6F sl 3 sts on to cable needle at front, k3, k3 from cable needle.

C6B sl 3 sts on to cable needle at back, k3, k3 from cable needle.

Cr4R sl 1 st on to cable needle at back, k3, p1 from cable needle.

Cr4L sl 3 sts on to cable needle at front, p1, k3 from cable needle.

Cr5R sl 2 sts on to cable needle at back, k3, p2 from cable needle.

Cr5L sl 3 sts on to cable needle at front, p2, k3 from cable needle.

C7F sl 4 sts on to cable needle at front, k3, sl p st back on to LH needle and p it, k3 from cable needle.

MB (make a bobble) (k1, p1) twice into next st and turn, p4 and turn, k4 and turn, p2tog, ssp and turn, k2tog.

The cables and bobbles add an individual touch to this bag (see page 110 for more information on making the cables). The strap also forms the sides and base of the bag. A tape is threaded through the strap, around the bag, adding strength and preventing it from stretching. A phone pocket is conveniently added onto the strap. The bag is lined with hard-wearing stiff denim to add structure and resilience.

Panel A (12 sts)
Row 1 RS P3, C6F, p3.
Row 2 K3, p6, k3.
Row 3 P1, Cr5R, Cr5L, P1.
Row 4 K1, P3, k4, p3, k1.
Row 5 Cr4R, p4, Cr4L.
Row 6 P3, k6, p3.
Row 7 K3, p6, k3.
Row 8 As row 6.
Row 9 Cr4L, p4, Cr4R.
Row 10 As row 4.
Row 11 P1, Cr5L, Cr5R, p1.
Row 12 As row 2.

Panel B (23 sts)
Row 1 RS P8, C7F, p8.
Row 2 K8, p3, k1, p3, k8.
Row 3 P6, Cr4R, p1, Cr4L, p6.
Row 4 K6, p3, k5, p3, k6.
Row 5 P4, Cr4R, p5, Cr4L, p4.
Row 6 K4, p3, k9, p3, k4.
Row 7 P2, Cr4R, p9, Cr4L, p2.
Row 8 K2, p3, k13, p3, k2.
Row 9 P1, Cr4R, p6, MB, p6, Cr4L, p1.
Row 10 K1, p3, k15, p3, k1.
Row 11 Cr4R, p15, Cr4L.
Row 12 P3, k17, p3.
Row 13 K3, (p5, MB) twice, p5, k3.
Row 14 As row 12.
Row 15 Cr4L, p15, Cr4R.
Row 16 As row 10.
Row 17 P1, Cr4L, p6, MB, p6, Cr4R, p1.
Row 18 As row 8.
Row 19 P2, Cr5L, p9, Cr5R, p2.
Row 20 As row 6.
Row 21 P4, Cr5L, p5, Cr5R, p4.
Row 22 As row 4.

Row 23 P6, Cr5L, p1, Cr5R, p6.
Row 24 As row 2.

Panel C (12 sts)
Row 1 RS P3, C6B, p3.
Rows 2 to 12 Work as given for panel A.

Knit your bag...
Flap and Back

Using size 7 (4.5mm) needles, cast on 65 sts.
Moss st (UK: double moss st) border
Row 1 RS K1, *p1, k1; rep from * to end.
Row 2 P1, *k1, p1; rep from * to end.
Row 3 As row 2.
Row 4 As row 1.
Row 5 As row 1.
Inc Row P1, (k1, p1) 3 times, (M1, k1, p1, k1, M1, p1, k1, p1) 9 times, (k1, p1) twice. 83 sts.
Commence cable patt.
**Foundation Row 1 (P1, k1) twice, k4, p5, k6, p5, k4, p10, k3, p1, k3, p10, k4, p5, k6, p5, k4, (k1, p1) twice.
Foundation Row 2 (K1, p1) twice, p3, k5, p6, k5, p4, k10, p3, k1, p3, k10, p4, k5, p6, k5, p4, (p1, k1) twice.
Row 1 (K1, p1) twice, C4F, p2, work row 1 of panel A, p2, C4B, p2, work row 1 of panel B, p2, C4F, p2, work row 1 of panel C, p2, C4B, (p1, k1) twice.
Row 2 (P1, k1) twice, p4, k2, work row 2 of panel C, k2, p4, k2, work row 2 of panel B, k2, p4, k2, work row 2 of panel A, k2, p4, (k1, p1) twice.
Row 3 (P1, k1) twice, k4, p2, work row 3 of panel A, p2, k4, p2, work row 3 of panel B, p2, k4, p2, work row 3 of panel C, p2, k4, (k1, p1) twice.
Row 4 (K1, p1) twice, p4, k2, work row 4 of panel C, k2, p4, k2, work row 4 of panel B, k2, p4, k2, work

row 4 of panel A, k2, p4, (p1, k1) twice.**

These 4 rows form moss st (UK: double moss st) borders and small cables, and set the panels A, B and C.

Cont in cable patt as set, commencing with row 5 of panels, until flap measures approx 11in (28cm) from beg, ending with row 14 of panel B.

Dec Row (P1, k1) 3 times, p1, (k2tog, p1, k1, p2tog, k1, p1) 9 times, (k1, p1) twice. 65 sts.

Cont in moss st (UK: double moss st) until back measures same length as Flap, ending with a RS row.

Bind off in patt.

Front

Using size 7 (4.5mm) needles, cast on 83 sts.

Commence cable patt.

Work as given for Flap from ** to ** but replace moss st (UK: double moss st) borders with rev st st – p first and last 4 sts on RS rows and k first and last 4 sts on WS rows.

OMITTING THE BOBBLES FROM PANEL B (work p1 instead of MB), cont in cable patt as set, commencing with row 5 of panels, until front measures approx 10in (25.5cm) from beg, ending with row 14 of panel B.

Dec Row (P1, k1) 3 times, p1, (k2tog, p1, k1, p2tog, k1, p1) 9 times, (k1, p1) twice. 65 sts.

Work 4 rows in moss st (UK: double moss st) as given for Flap.

Bind off in patt.

Gussets/strap (make 2)

Using size 7 (4.5mm) needles, cast on 8 sts.

Work in st st (1 row k, 1 row p) until gusset measures 11in (28cm) from beg. Place a marker at end of row.

Work another 14in (35.5cm) in st st from first marker and place second marker at end of row.

Work another 11in (28cm) in st st from second marker and place third marker at end of row.

Cont in st st until strap measures 45in (114.5cm) from third marker.

Bind off.

Pocket

Using size 7 (4.5mm) needles, cast on 14 sts.

Row 1 P1, k3, p6, k3, p1.

Row 2 K1, p3, k6, p3, k1.

Row 3 P1, work row 9 of panel C, p1.

Row 4 K1, work row 10 of panel C, k1.

Row 5 P1, work row 11 of panel C, p1.

Row 6 K1, work row 12 of panel C, k1.

Next Row Cast on 4 sts, p5 (including 4 sts just cast on), work row 1 of panel C, p1.

Next Row Cast on 4 sts, k5 (including 4 sts just cast on), work row 2 of panel C, k5. 22 sts.

Next Row P5, work row 3 of panel C, p5.

Next Row K5, work row 4 of panel C, k5.

Cont in cable patt as set, commencing with row 5 of panel C, until pocket measures approx 5in (12.5cm) from beg, ending with row 2 of panel C.

Dec Row (K1, p1) 3 times, k2tog, p1, k1, p2tog, k1, p1, k2tog, (p1, k1) 3 times. 19 sts.

Work 4 rows in moss st (UK: double moss st) as given for Flap.

Bind off in patt.

Pocket flap

Using size 7 (4.5mm) needles, cast on 11 sts.

Work 4 rows in moss st (UK: double moss st) as given for Flap.

Buttonhole Row Patt 5 sts, yo, k2tog, patt to end.

Cont in moss st (UK: double moss st) until flap measures 2½in (6cm) from beg, ending with a WS row.

Dec 1 st at each end of next row.

Patt 2 rows.

Bind off in patt.

to finish...

Sew in all ends. Press according to instructions on ball band.

Lining

Measure width and length of flap and back. Add a hem allowance of 1½in (4cm) onto each of these measurements. Draw a rectangle this size onto a piece of paper and cut out. Pin the paper pattern onto the lining fabric and cut out. Turn under 1in (2.5cm) on each edge and press. Pin the lining onto WS of flap and back, and slipstitch into position (there will be a small gap all the way round). Make up a lining for the front in the same way and sew in place. Take one gusset/strap and pin around the front, beginning at top left edge, matching first marker to bottom left corner, second one to right bottom corner and third one to right top edge. Try on bag and shorten or lengthen strap to length desired. Join ends of gusset and strap. Sew the other edge to the back in the same way. Join corners of pocket together. Place onto RS of strap 6in (15cm) above bag and sew pocket edges flat onto strap. Sew flap above it. Fold flap over and sew on button. With WS together, sew the second gusset/strap inside the first piece. Leave the end open. Thread the webbing through the strap and gussets. Cut to the right length and join ends together. Sew ends of strap together.

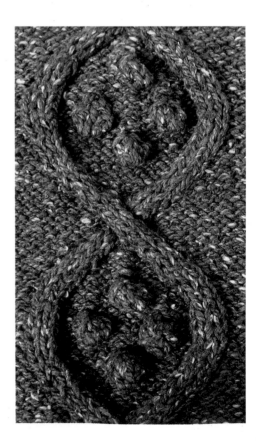

posy purses

Gardens are a great source of inspiration for fashion ideas – think how many floral fabrics we see every summer – and the pretty wrist bags featured in this section are inspired by two of the most popular flowers: daisies and roses. The fresh-looking daisy bag in vibrant cotton makes an ideal fun, everyday bag. The Rose Petal purse (see page 93), in a sophisticated pastel palette and lustrous silk yarn, makes a wrist bag suitable for a more special occasion.

DESIGN SECRETS UNRAVELLED…

Think of other flowers that you could create with this pattern. Knit the five petals in pink, yellow or hot orange. Change the background colour to a softer green or a different colour; sky blue or natural earth shades. How about adding another round of petals? Knit them the same size and attach at the base only; let the ends curl for a three-dimensional flower. Chose hot pink for a gerbera or mauve for a passionflower. Add another round of petals, smaller this time, and work in pale pink for a dahlia. Increase the petal to only nine or seven stitches and then decrease.

YARN FOCUS
The obvious yarn choice for this bag was mercerized cotton; it is crisp, fresh and creates a smooth fabric. The bright grass green is the perfect background for the pure white daisy petals and sunny yellow beads.

daisy days

MEASUREMENTS
Finished bag measures 5in (12.5cm)
in diameter; purse measures 3in (7.5cm)
wide and 2in (5cm) high

GATHER TOGETHER...
Materials
A 1 x 1¾oz (50g) ball of fine-weight (4ply)
cotton (125yd/115m per ball) in green

B 1 x 1¾oz (50g) ball of fine-weight (4ply)
cotton (125yd/115m per ball) in white

Needles and notions
1 pair of size 3 (3mm) needles
Self-cover button and a piece of yellow
fabric to cover it
Yellow beads
4in (10cm) zip for the purse

GAUGE
24 sts and 32 rows to 4in (10cm) measured over
st st using size 3 (3mm) needles and yarn A

Two circles, shaped using ssk, are sewn together to form this fun bag. A simple garter stitch wrist strap and loop close the bag. The petals are shaped using M1 and decreased to a point using ssk and k2tog (see pages 105 and 107). The accompanying purse is decorated with lazy daisies (see page 120) and fastened with a zip (see page 117). It is attached with a braided cord.

Knit your bag...
Back and Front (make 2 the same)
Using size 3 (3mm) needles and A, cast on 90 sts.
Row 1 and every foll WS row P to end.
Row 2 K1, (ssk, k9) 8 times, k1. 82 sts.
Row 4 K1, (ssk, k8) 8 times, k1. 74 sts.
Row 6 K1, (ssk, k7) 8 times, k1. 66 sts.
Row 8 K1, (ssk, k6) 8 times, k1. 58 sts.
Cont to dec as set, working 1 st less between decs to 10 sts.
Cut yarn and thread through rem sts. Pull up tight and fasten off.

Daisy petals (make 5)
Using size 3 (3mm) needles and B, cast on 3 sts.
Row 1 and every foll WS row P to end.
Row 2 K1, (M1, k1) twice. 5 sts.
Row 4 K2, M1, k1, M1, k2. 7 sts.
Row 6 K3, M1, k1, M1, k3. 9 sts.
Row 8 K4, M1, k1, M1, k4. 11 sts.
Row 10 Ssk, k7, k2tog. 9 sts.
Row 12 Ssk, k5, k2tog. 7 sts.
Row 14 Ssk, k3, k2tog. 5 sts.
Row 16 Ssk, k1, k2tog. 3 sts.
Row 18 Sk2po.
Cut yarn and thread through rem st.

Handle
Using size 3 (3mm) needles and A, cast on 60 sts.
Knit 2 rows.
Bind off.

Loop
Using size 3 (3mm) needles and A, cast on 20 sts.
Knit 2 rows.
Bind off.

Knit your purse...
Back and Front (make 2 the same)
Using size 3 (3mm) needles and A, cast on 18 sts.
Work 2in (5cm) in st st (1 row k, 1 row p), ending with a p row.
Bind off purlwise.

to finish...
Sew in all ends. Press according to instructions on ball band.
Draw around the covered button onto the yellow fabric. Sew yellow beads on to fill this circle. Make up the covered button according to the manufacturer's instructions. Sew the five petals onto the front to form a flower, placing the points to the outside edge. Sew the button into the centre. Place the front and back together with WS facing. Leaving a 4in (10cm) gap at the top, sew around the outside using a neat stabbing stitch as the stitching will be seen. Sew each end of the handle onto the top edge of the back 1in (2.5cm) apart. Sew each end of the loop onto the front 1in (2.5cm) apart. Cut three 10in (25.5cm) lengths of A. Braid them (see page 121) and attach one end to the inside of the bag on a side seam.

Purse
Using B, sew two or three lazy daisies (see page 120) on the front and back. Sew the zip into place along the front and back bound-off edges. If your zip is too long, sew several strong binding stitches around the zip teeth 4in (10cm) from the opening end. Then trim the excess length. Join the side and base seams, enclosing any extra zip length inside and sewing the end of the braid into a side seam at the top to attach the purse to the bag.

MEASUREMENTS

Finished bag measures 5in (12.5cm)
in diameter; purse measures 3in (7.5cm) wide
and 2in (5cm) high

GATHER TOGETHER…
Materials

A 1 x 1¾oz (50g) ball of fine-weight (4ply)
silk yarn (136yd/125m per ball) in pale green
B 1 x 1¾oz (50g) ball of fine-weight (4ply)
silk yarn (136yd/125m per ball) in pale yellow

Needles and notions

1 pair of size 6 (4mm) needles
Large feature button
4in (10cm) zip for the purse

GAUGE

24 sts and 32 rows to 4in (10cm) measured over
st st using size 6 (4mm) needles and yarn A

YARN FOCUS

I chose silk yarn to give this bag a soft, luxurious
feel; the silk adds a gentle sheen to the pale
colours. This bag doesn't have the structure that
the daisy bag has; instead it is reminiscent of
a large silk fabric corsage pinned to an elegant
evening dress. I knitted it on larger needles to
achieve the correct gauge.

This version is made up in exactly the same way as the Daisy Days bag; the only difference is the shape of the petals and the yarn used. Instead of pointed petals, the rose petals are wider with a flat end, and they are arranged in four layers. The petals in the top three layers are sewn down only at the points to allow the ends to curl up and create a wonderful deep bloom.

Knit your bag…
Back, Front, Handle, Loop and Purse
Work as given for Daisy Days.

Large rose petals (make 10)
Using size 6 (4mm) needles and B, cast on 3 sts.
Row 1 and every foll WS row P to end.
Row 2 K1, (M1, k1) twice. 5 sts.
Row 4 K2, M1, k1, M1, k2. 7 sts.
Row 6 K3, M1, k1, M1, k3. 9 sts.
Row 8 K4, M1, k1, M1, k4. 11 sts.
Row 10 K5, M1, k1, M1, k5. 13 sts.
Row 12 K6, M1, k1, M1, k6. 15 sts.
Row 14 Ssk, k11, k2tog. 13 sts.
Row 16 Ssk, k9, k2tog. 11 sts.
Row 18 Ssk, k7, k2tog. 9 sts.
Row 20 Ssk, k5, k2tog. 7 sts.
Bind off.

Small rose petals (make 10)
Work rows 1 to 11 as given for Large Rose Petals
(13 sts) and then rows 16 to 20.
Bind off.

to finish…
Sew in all ends. Press according to instructions
on ball band.
Sew five large petals onto the front to form a flower,
placing the flat ends to the outside edge so they
lie flat. Sew a second layer of five large petals on
top, placing each petal into the gap on the bottom
layer and leaving the ends free to curl up. Sew two
layers of five small petals each on top, alternating
positions as before, and securing the pointed ends
only. Sew the button into the centre. Finish rest of
bag and purse as given for Daisy Days.

DESIGN SECRETS UNRAVELLED…

The flatter petal shape can be used to knit many
more types of flowers; large brightly coloured
exotics or softer camellias and clematis. Grade
the colour from light to dark through the layers or
add a contrasting colour for the top layer only. Use
this bag in winter as well, working it in wool with
a bright silk flower, or chenille with petals in a soft
mohair mix yarn.

fabulous fair isle

The Fair Isle technique of coloured knitting is used to make this purse; traditional motifs are reworked in soft blues and a metallic green. The bag is mounted onto a decorative silver frame, which snaps closed and has tabs for a twisted cord handle or chain. This is a distinguished-looking purse that is worth spending some time and care over. The pattern has the ornate look of old-fashioned tapestries, while the addition of the silver frame gives the purse an elegant vintage feel.

Fair Isle knitting may seem a complex technique at first, but it is worth persevering with to achieve these fabulous colour motifs.

YARN FOCUS

I collected together a range of cottons and cotton mixes in shades of blue for the background, but cut it down to just four yarns: two cottons in light and dark denim marl, and a light and dark blue-violet. By combining them with each other, the bag looks more complicated than it is. I wanted to introduce a metallic yarn to carry on the theme of the metal frame. I found this wonderful pale sea-green yarn with a metallic thread; it has a marled effect and so merges with the marled background while contrasting well with the solid colours.

DESIGN SECRETS UNRAVELLED...

I have given a small cheat in the instructions; if you don't want to knit Fair Isle, you can knit the background and then embroider the pattern motifs on. This is much quicker and neater if you don't like working with two yarns at once. Although I used only four colours for the background, you could use more. Choose light and dark tones of the same colour for each pattern stripe. This purse would look fantastic in a range of fiery reds and oranges with a gold metallic pattern, mounted onto a gold frame. You could choose a sleeker, more modern frame and use contemporary fashion colours, such as aquas and browns, or pinks and lime greens.

classic colours

MEASUREMENTS
8½in (21.5cm) long, 6½in (16.5cm) wide at
top and 8in (20.5cm) at base

GATHER TOGETHER...
Materials
A 1 x 1¾oz (50g) ball of medium-weight (aran)
yarn with metallic thread (126yd/115m per ball)
in pale sea green
B 1 x 1¾oz (50g) ball of light-weight (DK)
cotton (115yd/106m per ball) in dark blue-violet
C 1 x 1¾oz (50g) ball of light-weight (DK)
cotton (104yd/95m per ball) in blue-violet
D 1 x 1¾oz (50g) ball of light-weight (DK)
cotton-mix yarn (104yd/95m per ball/hank)
in light denim blue marl
E 1 x 1¾oz (50g) ball of light-weight (DK)
cotton-mix yarn (104yd/95m per ball/hank)
in dark denim blue marl

Needles and notions
1 pair of size 6 (4mm) needles
Purse frame having a maximum internal
measurement of 6in (15cm)
Strong sewing thread in a colour to match
the frame

GAUGE
23 sts and 26 rows to 4in (10cm) measured over
Fair Isle pattern using size 6 (4mm) needles

I have offered you two methods of making this bag: you can either knit it using the Fair Isle technique (see below) or you can add the pattern using Swiss darning (see pages 98–99 and 120). This purse is structured with a metal purse frame (see page 119); these are available in a wide range of styles and finishes. The sides are decreased to give the bag its flared shape.

A note on technique...
Fair Isle is the technique of knitting with two colours in one row. Because you are using only two colours, you can use the yarn straight from the ball, without having to wind off bobbins as for intarsia (see pages 108–109). The unused colour is loosely carried along the back of the work behind the stitches in the working colour. This is called stranding. It is important that the stranded yarn is not pulled up too tightly; if it is, the knitted fabric will pucker and not lie flat. When you change colours, spread out the stitches just worked on the needle, pick up the new colour behind them and carry on knitting with the new colour.

Holding the colours
You can either hold both colours together in your hand or one at a time. To hold both colours, wrap both colours together over your right hand as you would do normally. Have the working yarn over the index finger; knit or purl the required number of stitches, then drop it off this finger and pick up the other colour with the finger. Use this to work the required number of stitches then swap colours in the same way. Always pick up the background colour (B, C, D or E) from under the pattern colour (A), and pick up the pattern colour over the background colour. This way the yarns won't become twisted.

To hold one yarn at a time, drop the working colour from your hand and pick up the new colour, wrapping around your hand as normal. See the note above about picking up the colours so they don't become twisted.

Knit your bag...
Front and Back (make 2 the same)
Using size 6 (4mm) needles and B, cast on 53 sts.
Commence chart.
Reading RS (odd) rows from right to left and WS (even) rows from left to right, and dec 1 st at each end of 9th and every foll 4th row to 39 sts, work in st st until row 56 has been completed.
Bind off.

to finish...
Sew in all ends. Press according to instructions on ball bands.

Lining

Use the front to make a simple lining for a shaped bag (page 115).

Sewing in the purse frame

Divide the top edge of each of the knitted pieces into quarters; place a marker in the centre stitch at the top edge, fold each corner to the centre and place a marker on the folds. Open purse frame. If using a curved frame, place a pin through the hole at the natural corner. A square frame will have an obvious corner. Place a pin through the centre hole on the frame's top edge. Count the holes between the corner pins and centre pin and place a pin to divide in half. Match these pins to the corners and markers on the front. Thread a sharp needle. Secure the strong sewing thread to the centre stitch, take the needle up through the centre hole

on the frame, down through the hole to its right and down through the knitted fabric. Bring it up through the knitting and up through the next hole along. Continue in this way to the corner, easing in any excess fabric as you sew. Work back along the line of stitches on the frame, filling in every other stitch to produce a continuous line of stitches. Secure thread at the centre and repeat for the other side. Turn the work and frame over and do the same with the other knitted piece.

Sew the side edges into the frame in the same way, making sure the fabric is neither stretched nor pulling in. Join each side edge from the base to the frame. Join the base seam. Push the corners in and, on the WS, sew across the points 1in (2.5cm) from the tip.

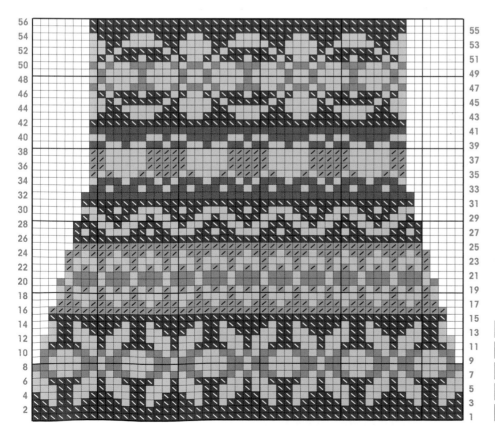

	A
⟍	B
	C
∕	D
	E

retro revamp

MEASUREMENTS

8½in (21.5cm) long, 7½in (19cm) wide at
top and 10½in (26cm) at base

GATHER TOGETHER...

Materials

A 1 x ⅞oz (25g) ball of fine-weight (4ply)
metallic yarn (218yd/200m per ball) in gold

B 1 x 1¾oz (50g) ball of light-weight (DK) cotton
(93yd/85m per ball) in red

C 1 x 1¾oz (50g) ball of medium-weight (aran)
cotton-mix yarn (118yd/108m per ball)
in salmon red

D 1 x 1¾oz (50g) ball of light-weight (DK) cotton
(125yd/115m per ball) in light orange

E 1 x 1¾oz (50g) ball of light-weight (DK) cotton
(92yd/84m per ball) in orange

Needles and notions

1 pair of size 6 (4mm) needles
Beaded handle
Lining fabric 9¾in (24.5cm) x 18½in (47cm)

GAUGE

20 sts and 28 rows to 4in (10cm) measured over
st st using size 6 (4mm) needles and yarn B

*Knit note: This bag has the pattern added by
using Swiss darning. This is an embroidery stitch
that mimics the knitted stitches. It could also be
knitted using the Fair Isle technique (see details
on page 96).*

As an alternative to knitting Fair Isle, you can embroider the pattern on using Swiss darning (page 120). The background is knitted first; follow the chart, omitting the pattern, and you end up with a striped fabric. The pattern is added to the front only, with the back left as a fiery mix of red and orange stripes. Although the same shape as the blue version, this has a totally different look with a beaded handle that echoes the colours of the knitting. And because you are not stranding yarn over the back of the fabric, the gauge is looser, making the bag slightly bigger.

Front and Back (make 2 the same)

Using size 6 (4mm) needles and B, cast on 53 sts.
Commence chart, working only the background colours (B, C, D and E) and omitting the pattern in A, work these stitches in the background colour on which they lie:
read RS (odd) rows from right to left and WS (even) rows from left to right, and dec 1 st at each end of 9th and every foll 4th row to 39 sts, work in st st (1 row K, 1 row P) until row 56 has been completed.

Turning Row Using B, purl to end.
Using B, work 4 rows in st st, starting with a P row.
Bind off.

to finish...

Sew in all ends. Press according to instructions on ball bands.

Lining

Use the front to make a simple lining for a shaped bag (page 115).
Working from the chart and using 2 strands of A, Swiss darn (see page 120) the pattern onto the front only.
Join side seams and base seam. Fold the facing over along the top edge and slipstitch into place. Attach the handle at each side seam. With WS together, slip the lining into the bag and slipstitch neatly into place around top of bag.

YARN FOCUS

This is a really hot palette of colours: red, orange and gold. I chose two shades of red, a deep red and a lighter salmon red, to contrast with a bright clear tangerine and a deeper, more spicy, orange. Even just using one fibre, I have a mix of textures; crisp mercerized cotton, smooth matte cotton and a rough cotton/silk mix all add interest to the knitted fabric. The metallic gold yarn is crunchy and hard, and adds another texture to the mix. Swiss darning can cover the background stitches completely; I used two strands of a thin yarn for the embroidery and so some of the background showed through the pattern. I like this 'imperfect' effect because it blends the colours together and the pattern becomes part of the background instead of standing apart on top.

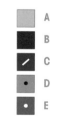

A
B
C
D
E

DESIGN SECRETS UNRAVELLED...

The blue version of this bag is soft and classic, while the red version is bright and modern: a whole new look has been created just by changing the colour palette and handle. How about using traditional tweed wool in heather and earth shades with the pattern in mustard for seasonal colour? Or you could try the richness of silk in purples and mauves with a deep burgundy for opulence. Just chose two complementary sets of colours, a dark and light shade in each, and a contrasting colour for the pattern. Go for light-weight (DK) yarns – although I also used a medium-weight (aran) yarn for the colour: the thicker yarn added texture to the mix.

it's all in the detail...

casting on

Most knitters have their own favoured way of casting on, so I have not specified in the projects which method to use. However, several of the bags are shaped by casting on stitches at the beginning of a row; the Off the Cuff bag (pages 32–35) and the Buttons and Bows bag (pages 82–85) are both shaped in this way. You should use the cable cast-on for this. It is also used extensively for the Square Dance bag (pages 68–71), where cable cast-on is used to form the shapes. Cable cast-on is also used for working buttonholes, which are used for fastenings and attaching straps. You can, of course, use it to cast on stitches at the beginning of a project; it makes a very firm, strong edge, making it ideal for bags. This method needs two needles.

BUTTONHOLES

All the buttonholes used on the bags are worked over two rows. On the first row, two or three stitches are bound off. On the second row, work up to the bound-off stitches, turn the work and cast on the same number of stitches using the cable cast-on, working the first stitch between the last two stitches worked on the left-hand needle. Turn the work back and continue along the row.

CABLE CAST-ON

To cast on at the beginning of a project, make a slip knot about 6in (15cm) from the end of the yarn and slip it on to a needle held in your left hand.

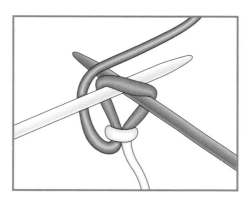

1 Insert the right-hand needle into the slip knot as though to knit it and wrap the yarn around the tip.

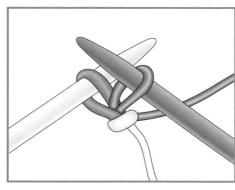

2 Pull a new loop through but do not slip the stitch off the left-hand needle.

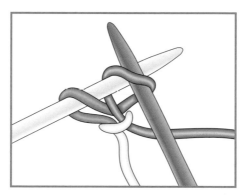

3 Place the loop on to the left-hand needle by inserting the left-hand needle into the front of the loop from right to left.

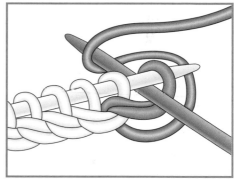

4 Insert the right-hand needle between the two stitches and wrap the yarn around the tip. When the new loop is pulled through between the stitches, place it on the left-hand needle, as shown in step 3. Repeat step 4 until you have cast on the required number of stitches.

Extra stitches

To cast on the extra stitches needed in the middle of knitting, work step 4 only, working the first stitch between the next two stitches already on the left-hand needle.

knit stitch

In knitting there are only two stitches to learn: knit (k) and purl (p). All other knitted fabrics are created by combining these two stitches. The knit stitch is the one that all beginners learn first and is very versatile when used on its own. When you knit each row, the fabric you make is garter stitch. It lies flat, is quite a thick fabric and does not curl at the edges, which is why I have used it for handles and as an edging on several bags, including the Patching It Up bag (pages 28–31).

MAKING THE KNIT STITCH

Each knit stitch is made up of four easy steps. The yarn is held at the back of the work (the side facing away from you).

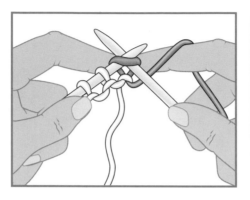

1 Hold the needle with the cast-on stitches in your left hand, and insert the right-hand needle into the front of the stitch from left to right.

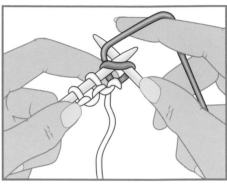

2 Pass the yarn under and around the right-hand needle.

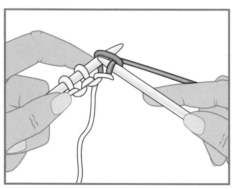

3 Pull the new loop on the right-hand needle through the stitch on the left-hand needle.

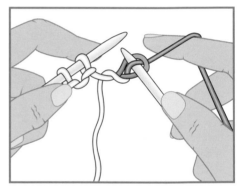

4 Slip the stitch off the left-hand needle. One knit stitch is completed.

Repeat these four steps for each stitch on the left-hand needle. All the stitches on the left-hand needle will be transferred to the right-hand needle, where the new row is formed. At the end of the row, swap the needle with the stitches into your left hand and the empty needle into your right hand to begin the next row.

purl stitch

Purl stitch is just as easy to learn as knit stitch. Once you know both stitches, you can pretty much make anything. One row of knit and one row of purl makes stockinette stitch. The Simply Chic bags (pages 20–27) are a great way to practise your knit and purl; just cast on, work in stockinette stitch and bind off.

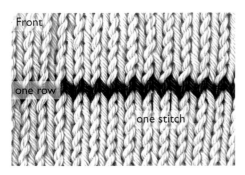

STOCKINETTE STITCH

Stockinette stitch (st st) is formed by knitting one row, purling the next row, and then repeating these two rows.

In the knitting instructions for the projects, stockinette stitch is written as follows:

Row 1 RS Knit.

Row 2 Purl.

Or, the instructions may be:

Work in st st (1 row k, 1 row p), beg with a k row.

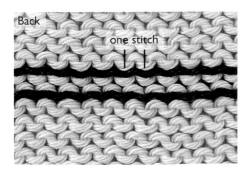

REVERSE STOCKINETTE STITCH

Reverse stockinette stitch (rev st st) is when the back of stockinette stitch fabric is used as the right side. This is commonly used as the background for cables, but can also be used as the right side of fabrics knitted in fancy yarns, such as faux fur or fashion yarns. This is because most of the textured effect of the yarn remains on the reverse side of the fabric.

MAKING THE PURL STITCH

Each purl stitch is made up of four easy steps. The yarn is held at the front of the work (the side facing you).

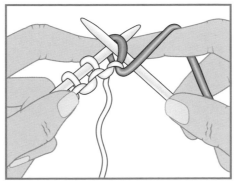

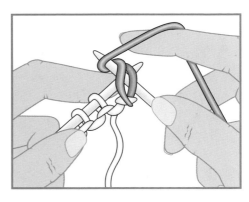

1 Hold the needle with the cast-on stitches in your left hand, and insert the right-hand needle into the front of the stitch from right to left.

2 Pass the yarn over and around the right-hand needle.

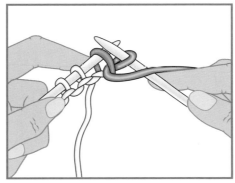

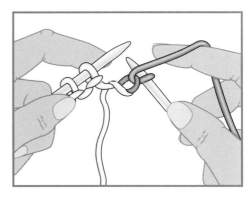

3 Pull the new loop on the right-hand needle through the stitch on the left-hand needle.

4 Slip the stitch off the left-hand needle. One stitch is completed.

Repeat these four steps for each stitch on the left-hand needle. All the stitches on the left-hand needle will be transferred to the right-hand needle, where the new purl row is formed. At the end of the row, swap the needle with the stitches into your left hand and the empty needle into your right hand to begin the next row.

binding off

Unless specifically instructed to do otherwise, you should bind off in pattern – for example, knitwise on the right side of a piece knitted in stockinette stitch. The various methods are explained right and below. The bound-off edge should not be too tight, otherwise it will pull the knitted fabric in. This is important when binding off an edge that will show, such as the top of a bag or edge of a pocket. If you tend to bind off tightly, try using a needle a size larger than that used for the knitted fabric.

KNIT PERFECT

When you wish to stop knitting, but aren't ready to bind off yet, always finish the complete row. Finishing in the middle of a row will stretch the stitches and they may slide off the needle. If you need to put your knitting aside for several weeks or even months and do not have time to finish the piece beforehand, mark on the pattern or make a note of where you have got to. If you are working in a regular pattern such as stockinette stitch, when restarting again it is worth unravelling a couple of rows and reknitting them, as stitches left over time on the needles can become stretched and leave an unsightly ridge where you stopped.

BIND OFF KNITWISE

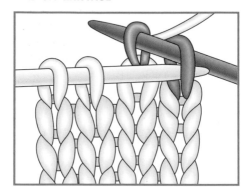

1 Knit two stitches, and insert the tip of the left-hand needle into the front of the first stitch on the right-hand needle.

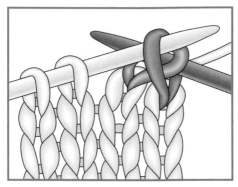

2 Lift this stitch over the second stitch and off the needle.

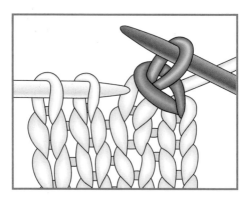

3 One stitch is left on the right-hand needle.

4 Knit the next stitch and lift the second stitch over this and off the needle. Continue in this way until one stitch remains on the right-hand needle.

Cut the yarn (leaving a length long enough to sew in), thread the end through the last stitch and slip it off the needle. Pull the yarn end to tighten the stitch.

BIND OFF PURLWISE

To bind off on a purl row, simply purl the stitches instead of knitting them.

BIND OFF IN PATTERN

To bind off in a pattern such as rib, you must knit the knit stitches and purl the purl stitches of the rib. If you are working a pattern of cable stitches, you bind off in pattern; again, knit the knit stitches and purl the purl stitches.

increasing stitches

Many of the bags in this book are shaped, and their shape is changed by increasing or decreasing stitches. The Buttons and Bows bag (pages 82–85) has increase stitches at each side to produce a lovely curve; these stitches are then decreased again at the top. The Get Back backpack (pages 36–39) has decrease stitches at each side to give it a flared shape. There are a few different ways to increase stitches. In some instructions, I have specified which increase to use, in others I haven't. Try to keep your increase edge as neat as possible; some of these edges will be seen on the finished bag. It always looks neater if the increase stitch is worked one stitch in from the edge.

MAKE 1 (M1)

This increase is used for shaping the petals on the Daisy Days bag (pages 90–92). It could also be used for increasing at side edges; work it one stitch in from the edge. Use both the right- and left-twisting versions for a neat finish. The new stitch is made between two existing stitches using the horizontal thread that lies between them.

To twist M1 to the left

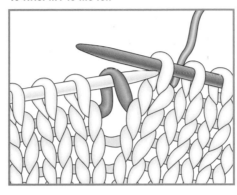

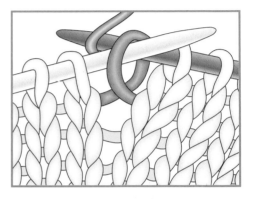

1 Knit to the point where the increase is to be made. Insert the tip of the left-hand needle under the running thread from front to back.

2 Knit this loop through the back to twist it. By twisting it you prevent a hole appearing where the made stitch is.

To twist M1 to the right

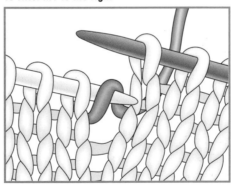

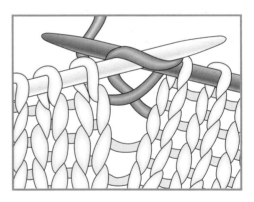

1 Knit to the point where the increase is to be made. Insert the tip of the left-hand needle under the running thread from back to front.

2 Knit this loop through the front to twist it.

increasing stitches

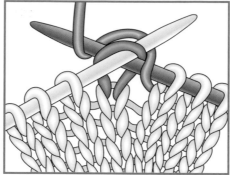

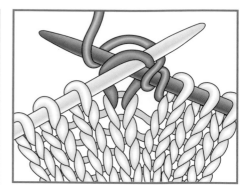

KNIT INTO FRONT AND BACK (KF&B)
Knit into the front of the stitch as usual. Do not slip the stitch off the left-hand needle, but knit into it again through the back of the loop. Then slip the original stitch off the left-hand needle.

PURL INTO FRONT AND BACK (PF&B)
Work as given for kf&b, but purl into the front and back instead.

YO (YFWD) BETWEEN TWO STITCHES
This produces a hole so is used for small buttonholes, or as a decorative increase such as on leaves. Bring the yarn forward between the two needles. Knit the next stitch, taking the yarn over the right hand needle.

MULTIPLE YARN OVERS
These are used to make the bigger holes in the Summertime Sweetie lace bag (pages 46–48).

YO TWICE
Wrap the yarn around the needle twice. On the return row, knit then purl into the 2-yo.

YO 3 TIMES
Wrap the yarn around the needle three times. On the return row, work as given in the pattern instructions.

The intricate patterns of lace knitting are created by using single and multiple yarnovers, as in the Summertime Sweetie bag.

decreasing stitches

Decreases are used on many of the bags, either to shape the bag or a detail of it. They are also used in stitch patterns and to form buttonholes.

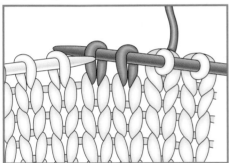

DECREASING ONE STITCH

There are a number of ways to decrease one stitch.

K2tog

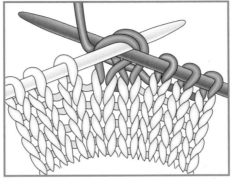

Knit to where the decrease is to be, insert the right-hand needle (as though to knit) through the next two stitches and knit them together as one stitch.

P2tog

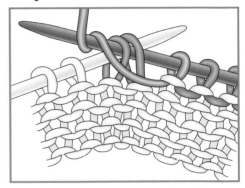

Purl to where the decrease is to be, insert the right-hand needle (as though to purl) through the next two stitches and purl them together as one stitch.

ssk or k2tog tbl

1 Slip two stitches knitwise one at a time from left-hand needle to right-hand needle (they will be twisted).

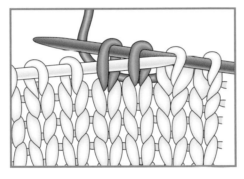

2 Insert the left-hand needle from left to right through the fronts of these two stitches and knit together as one stitch.

DECREASING TWO STITCHES AT ONCE

There are various ways of decreasing two stitches at once.

K3tog

Work as k2tog, but knit three stitches together instead of two.

P3tog

Work as p2tog, but purl three stitches together instead of two.

K3tog tbl

Work as ssk (or k2tog tbl), but slip three stitches instead of two and knit them together.

P3tog tbl

Work as ssp, but slip three stitches instead of two and purl them together through the backs of the loops.

SK2PO

This stands for: slip one, knit two together, pass slipped stitch over. Slip the next stitch onto the right-hand needle, knit the next two stitches together, and lift the slipped stitch over the k2tog and off the needle.

ssp

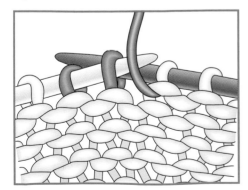

1 Slip two stitches knitwise, one at a time, from the left-hand needle to the right-hand needle (they will be twisted), pass these two stitches back to the left-hand needle in this twisted way.

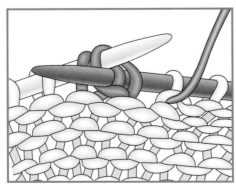

2 Purl these two stitches together through the back loops.

intarsia

Intarsia is the technique of colour knitting suitable for large blocks of colour or single motifs. Unlike Fair Isle knitting, where the yarn is stranded across the back of the work from one area to another, intarsia uses a separate ball or bobbin of colour for each block. The When the Cows Come Home bag (pages 60–63) has large areas of black and white and each is knitted using a separate bobbin. The Fantastic Flowers bag (pages 78–81) is the same; each flower has a separate bobbin and so does each area of background colour between them. When you change from one colour to another, you need to twist the yarns together to prevent a hole appearing.

BOBBINS

You should never knit straight from the ball, unless the design is very simple with only two or three colour changes on each row. With each colour change, the yarns are twisted and they will become tangled and the knitting become a chore. If you use bobbins, you can leave them hanging at the back of the work out of the way of other yarns.

You can buy plastic bobbins for intarsia, but it is easy to make your own. Leaving a long end, wind the yarn in a figure of eight around your thumb and little finger. Wind on sufficient to complete the area

to be knitted. Cut the yarn and use this cut end to tie a knot around the middle of the bobbin. Use the long end to pull the yarn from the centre of the bobbin.

TIDYING UP ENDS

There will be a lot of ends where colours have begun or ended. You should weave these in as you knit or sew them in every ten rows or so. This removes them from the back where they may become tangled with the working yarns. It also means that you won't have them to tidy up when you've finished knitting and want to get on with making up your bag.

Weaving in ends on a knit row

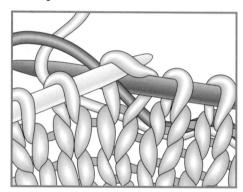

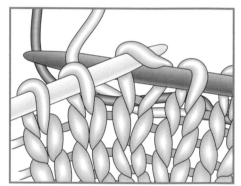

1 Insert the tip of the right-hand needle into the next stitch, bring the cut end over the needle, wrap the yarn around the needle as though to knit.

2 Pull the cut end off the needle and finish knitting the stitch. The cut end is caught into the knitted stitch.

Work the next stitch as normal, then catch the cut end in as before. If you work alternately like this the cut end will lie above and below the row of stitches.

Weaving in ends on a purl row

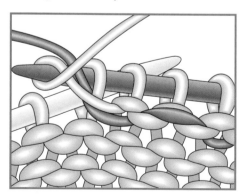

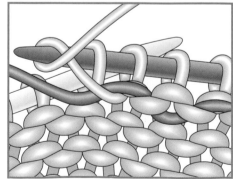

1 Insert the tip of the right-hand needle into the next stitch, bring the cut end over the needle, wrap the yarn around the needle as though to purl.

2 Pull the cut end off the needle and finish purling the stitch. The cut end is caught into the purled stitch.

Work the next stitch as normal, then catch the cut end in as before. If you work alternately like this the cut end will lie above and below the row of stitches.

JOINING IN NEW COLOURS

Knit to where the new colour begins, drop the old colour and pick up a bobbin of new colour. Knit the first stitch with it, then take the cut end and twist it once around the old colour. Weave it in with the new yarn.

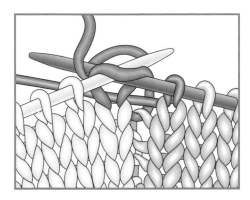
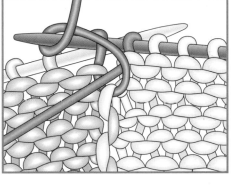

TWISTING YARNS TOGETHER

Once you've joined in all the colours that you need across the row, on the return row the yarns must be twisted to join the blocks of colour together. When you change colour, always pick up the new colour from under the old colour.

WORKING FROM CHARTS

Intarsia patterns are worked from charts. One square represents one stitch and a line of stitches represents one row. The rows are numbered: knit rows (RS rows) are odd numbers and are read from right to left; purl rows (WS rows) are even numbers and are read from left to right. Start knitting from the bottom right-hand corner of the chart at row 1.

The blocks of contrasting colours that make up the funky cow-print pattern of this bag are created using intarsia.

cables

Cables are simply a way of twisting two sets of stitches to form a rope or for carrying stitches across the fabric. Use a cable needle to hold the stitches or a double-pointed needle if you find a cable needle too short to hold.

C6F (CABLE SIX FRONT)

Work as C4F, but slip three stitches on to a cable needle instead of two and hold at front of work, and then knit three stitches.

C6B (CABLE SIX BACK)

Work as C4B, but slip three stitches on to a cable needle instead of two and hold at back of work, and then knit three stitches.

C7F (CABLE SEVEN FRONT)

1 Slip the next four stitches from the left-hand needle on to a cable needle and hold at the front of the work.
2 Knit the next three stitches on the left-hand needle.
3 Slip the purl stitch (the last stitch) from the cable needle back onto the left-hand needle and purl it.
4 Knit remaining three stitches from cable needle.

CR4R (CROSS FOUR RIGHT)

1 Slip the next stitch from the left-hand needle on to a cable needle and hold at the back of the work.
2 Knit the next three stitches on the left-hand needle, then purl the stitch from the cable needle.

CR4L (CROSS FOUR LEFT)

1 Slip the next three stitches from the left-hand needle on to a cable needle and hold at the front of the work.
2 Purl the next stitch on the left-hand needle, then knit the three stitches from the cable needle.

CR5R (CROSS FIVE RIGHT)

Work as Cr4R, but slip two stitches on to a cable needle at back of work, then knit the next three stitches on left-hand needle, before purling the two stitches from the cable needle.

CR5L (CROSS FIVE LEFT)

Work as Cr4L, slipping three stitches on to a cable needle at front of work, but then purl the next two stitches on the left-hand needle, before knitting the three stitches from the cable needle.

C4F (CABLE FOUR FRONT)

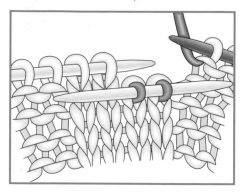

1 Slip the next two stitches from the left-hand needle on to a cable needle and hold at the front of the work.

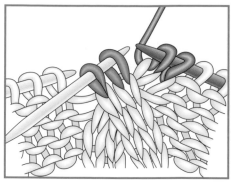

2 Knit the next two stitches on the left-hand needle, then knit the two stitches from the cable needle.

C4B (CABLE FOUR BACK)

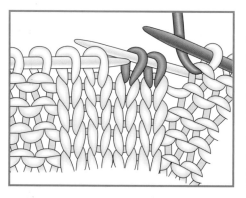

1 Slip the next two stitches from the left-hand needle on to a cable needle and hold at the back of the work.

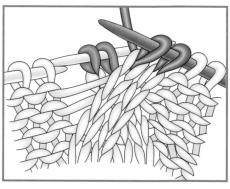

2 Knit the next two stitches on the left-hand needle, then knit the two stitches from the cable needle.

KNIT PERFECT

Use a row counter or mark on paper each row worked to keep track of the rows between twists of the cable. To count the rows between twists of a cable, look for the row where you worked the twist; you will be able to identify this by following the path of the yarn from the last stitch of the cable to the first background stitch for a front-cross cable or from the last background stitch to the first stitch of the cable for a back-cross cable. On the row below this there will be no connecting strand of yarn between these same stitches. Count each strand for every row above the twist row.

fulling

Fulling will give your bag more structure and strengthen handles and straps. Bags are small enough to full by hand (it is also possible to full items in a washing machine). Doing it by hand means that you will have more control over the process and be able to concentrate on areas that you want to full more, such as straps or handles. I've fulled the Square Dance bag (pages 68–71) and the Falling Leaves bag (pages 42–45).

KNIT PERFECT

Always test samples of multi-coloured knitting to make sure all the yarns are colourfast.

Fulling only works on 100% wool; work a sample before you knit your project to make sure your yarn will full.

Brush the surface of the knitting when dry with a stiff brush; use a gently pulling or lifting action rather than a vigorous back-and-forwards motion.

THE PROCESS OF FULLING

Fulling is the process of washing woollen fabric to produce a felt-like fabric. It is often mistakenly called felting; however, felting is worked on carded unspun wool, whereas fulling is worked on a finished fabric. Fulling can only be done on yarns that are 100% wool; it doesn't work on synthetics, cotton or wools that have been treated to be machine-washable. During fulling, the wool expands, fibres mesh together and individual stitches close up to form a soft fabric with a brushed appearance. The finished fabric will also shrink by up to 10% in length and width, although this varies with yarn and length of fulling. This means you should always knit an item you intend to full bigger than you want the finished item. Do a test sample before fulling your knitted item; measure the sample so you can see how much it shrinks. The two bags that I fulled are worked to different degrees. The Square Dance bag is fulled so that the colours merge together and the fabric becomes thick and fuzzy. But I wanted to keep the three-dimensional look of the stitches on the Falling Leaves bag, so I fulled it only until the stitches began to close up (although I fulled the handle more). Keep looking at your bag during the fulling process to check you are achieving the required effect or that the bag is the size you want.

HAND FULLING

Fulling depends on extremes of temperature, going from hot to cold, agitation by kneading and the use of soap; I use an olive-oil soap. Do not use detergent or washing powder. Immerse the sample in hot (not boiling) water, using gloves to protect your hands. Rub the sample with the soap and start kneading the fabric without pulling, stretching or rubbing the knitting together. Remove the sample from the water frequently to check the fulling process. Rinse the soap out in cold water and pull the sample gently. If the stitches still move apart easily, continue the fulling. Keep up the temperature of the hot water. Stop when the fabric is dense and has a fuzzy appearance. Rinse the soap out and squeeze (do not wring) to remove excess water. Roll the sample up in a towel to soak up any remaining moisture and then lay it out flat, away from direct heat, to dry. Measure it and compare with the previous measurements; this will give you a guide to how much your knitted item will shrink.

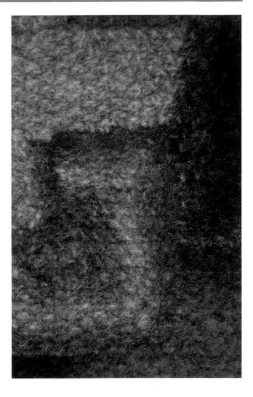

FULLING BAGS

Fulling should be done after the handles, pockets and knitted pieces have been put together and before adding things like zips, buttons, embellishments and linings. When the bag has been successfully fulled and is the required size, rinse, squeeze out the excess water and roll in a towel to soak up any remaining moisture. Pull the bag into shape, straightening seams and edges, and sharpening corners. If it is an unstructured or soft bag, I push a plastic bag into it and fill this with scrunched-up newspaper. This holds the bag apart and stops creases forming. Place it away from direct heat to dry. If the bag has a flat base or a gusset between the back and front, you will need to put something inside it so that it will dry to the correct shape. I sometimes use books, either one or a pile of them; make sure they are well wrapped in a plastic bag and slip them into the bag. Stand the bag on its base to dry; if you have to lay it down, keep turning frequently so the knitted fabric isn't crushed. You could also use a cardboard box if you find one the correct size, or pieces of card cut to shape. Make sure whatever you use isn't going to bleed colour when it becomes damp; if in doubt, line the bag with a plastic bag.

finishing

When you have finished knitting all the pieces for your project, you should press them before making up. The knitted pieces will look flatter and you can pull out any side edges so that they are straight. Before pressing, sew in all yarn ends but don't trim them. During pressing, the knitting will stretch and yarn ends can pull through. Wait until the pieces have been pressed.

STEAM PRESSING

This is the method that I use most for natural yarns, such as pure wool or yarns with a high wool content. Some yarns with a high synthetic fibre content such as polyester and nylon will not stand the high temperature needed for steaming, so should never be steamed. Always check the ball band before steaming or test on your gauge square first.

Using rustproof pins, pin the knitted piece out, wrong side up, onto an ironing board. If the piece is too big, like some of the larger bags or a long strap, make a pressing board from a folded blanket covered with a sheet. Lay a clean cotton cloth over the pinned-out piece to protect it. Set the steam iron on an appropriate heat setting for the yarn. Hold the iron close to the surface of the knitting without touching it. Do not press the iron on to the knitted fabric. Let the steam penetrate the fabric. Remove the cloth and allow the fabric to dry before unpinning.

WET PRESSING

This is an alternative to steam pressing and is better for synthetics or fancy yarns. Pin out the pieces onto a pressing board, as above. Wet a clean cotton cloth and wring out the excess water until it is just damp. Place it over the pinned-out piece and leave to dry away from direct heat. When the cloth is completely dry, remove it. Make sure the knitted pieces are also dry before you take out the pins and remove them from the board.

SEWING UP

Whenever possible, sew the pieces together with the yarn they are knitted from. If the yarn is something that will break easily or is textured, such as an eyelash yarn or bouclé, use a plain yarn in a matching colour. Do not use the long ends left after knitting the pieces to sew up with; if you do use them and you have to unpick the item for any reason, the ends may start to unravel the knitting. Use a tapestry needle and an 18in (45cm) length of yarn, so the yarn doesn't fray by being passed through the fabric too frequently.

Mattress stitch

To get an invisible seam, use mattress stitch. This is worked from the right side, making it easier to match stripes and shaping details, such as on the sides of bags. Secure the sewing yarn by weaving it down the edge of one of the pieces, bringing it to the front on the first row between the corner and second stitches. Place the two pieces to be joined side by side on a flat surface.

Joining two pieces of stockinette stitch

Having secured the yarn, take the needle across to the opposite side and insert it into the first row between the first and second stitches from front to back, take it under the horizontal strand of the row above and pull the yarn through. Take the needle across to the first edge, insert the needle into the first row between stitches again from front to back, and take it under the horizontal strands of the two rows above. Pull the yarn through. Insert the needle into the opposite edge again, in the same hole that the yarn came out of, and take it under the horizontal strands of the two rows above. Continue zigzagging between the edges, working under two rows each time. Pull the yarn up every few stitches to draw the seam together, but not too tightly – the seam should not pucker the fabric.

Joining two pieces of reverse stockinette stitch

Having secured the yarn, take the needle across to the opposite side and insert it from front to back under the horizontal strand of the row above and pull the yarn through. Take the needle across to the other edge and insert it from front to back under the top loop of the second stitch. Take the needle back to the other edge and work under the strand of the row above. Continue in this way, inserting the needle under the top loop of the second stitch on one edge and under the horizontal strand between the first and second stitches on the other edge. One side of the seam takes in one and a half stitches and the other takes in one stitch, but this weaves the rev st st together so the seam is invisible.

SEAMS ON THE RIGHT SIDE

I've used this method to sew on the pockets on the Belt Up bags (pages 50–55) and also to attach the flap on the Buttons and Bows bag (pages 82–85).

Lay the two pieces to be joined together as described in the project instructions. Sew through both thicknesses, one stitch in from the edge, using a small neat running stitch. You can use the knitted fabric as a guide to keep your stitches regular; sew over one stitch and under the next, or over one row and under the next. Do not pull the stitches too tightly or the fabric will pucker.

PICKING UP STITCHES

One piece of knitting can be joined to another by picking up stitches and using these instead of casting them on. This eliminates a seam and makes a smoother join. The stitches for the flap on the Get Back backpack (pages 36–39) have been picked up from the back.

Hold the work in your left hand with the right side facing. With a needle and the yarn in your right hand, insert the needle under the top of the loop of the first stitch. Wrap the yarn knitwise around the needle and draw through a loop. Continue in this way, inserting the needle under the top loop of each stitch until you have the correct number of stitches.

linings

Adding a lining to your bag will make it stronger, more hard-wearing and will prevent the bag from stretching when full. It will also cover the wrong side of the knitted fabric, which is especially useful for bags knitted using intarsia or Fair Isle. For structured bags, you can use the lining to add stiffness, while lined soft bags will hold their shape when full. Bags with a flat base need the base to be stiffened to hold the gussets open and keep the depth of the bag.

The Patching It Up bag (see pages 28–31) is unshaped so uses a simple lining, which is hard-wearing and will protect your bag.

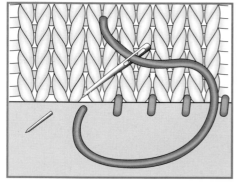

SLIPSTITCH

This is used for sewing the lining into a knitted bag. Fold the seam allowance to the WS around the top of the lining and press. Slip the lining into the knitted bag, matching any seams. Thread a sharp needle with strong sewing cotton in a colour to match the lining. Secure the end of the cotton to the lining at a seam. Take the needle under a knitted stitch and bring it back through the lining from WS to RS close to the folded edge. Take the needle under the next knitted stitch and bring back through the lining. Pull the small stitches taut but not so tightly that the lining puckers. Repeat these steps all around the lining, keeping the stitches small and spaced evenly.

FABRICS

The best lining fabric is cotton; this is easy to cut out and sew together, washes well if it becomes stained, and is hard-wearing, with no silky threads to catch on the contents of your bag. I often use patchwork cottons. These are available in such a wide range of colours that I can easily find one to complement any bag; the Frills and Spills bag (pages 64–66), for example, has a brilliant green cotton lining. Other fabrics to use for everyday bags are denim, canvas and calico. I used a heavy-weight denim to line the Instant Messenger bag (pages 86–89); it makes it very robust and the stiffness of the denim adds structure to the bag and the flap. I used calico for the When the Cows Come Home bag (pages 60–63) because it is lighter but still durable. It also has a lovely natural feel to it with flecks of fibre in the fabric.

Some bags, however, need a more luxurious lining. I used a grey silk for the Off the Cuff bag (pages 32–35) because it carried on the tailoring theme. The Pretty in Purple lace shoulder bag (page 49) has a rich purple satin for a lining. This one is seen through the lace so had to be extra-special. If your bag is just for a special occasion, such as a wedding, you could use silk or satin; the Always the Bridesmaid bag (page 24) could be lined with the same fabric as the bride or bridesmaid's dress. Evening bags can have softer linings. A silk yarn needs a silk fabric, while metallic and rayon would look fantastic lined with satin.

COLOURS

Many bought bags have a black lining; it is practical and inexpensive for manufacturers. Thankfully, we are not confined by such considerations. You should think of the lining as part of the bag's design. Try to match the colour of your yarn – this is where patchwork fabrics are so great. Alternatively, you could choose a contrasting colour for a fun twist. Or use a patterned fabric; multi-coloured stripes or playful polka dots. Small floral patterns would look fresh and light inside a summer bag. Felt or boiled wool fabric (look through the patchwork fabrics again) would make a tweed bag cosy and warming for winter.

A SIMPLE LINING FOR AN UNSHAPED BAG

Simple linings are for bags that have only two pieces; a front and back sewn together, with no base or gussets. The linings for the Simply Chic bags (pages 20–27) are made like this, as is the lining for the Patching It Up bag (pages 28–31).

YOU WILL NEED
pencil
set square
ruler
paper (lining paper is ideal)
pins
sewing thread
lining fabric

1 Press your knitted pieces to size, making sure the edges are straight and the corners square. The back and front should be the same size.

2 Measure the length and width of the front. Draw a square or rectangle onto the paper using these measurements. Add a seam allowance of ⅞in (1.5cm) onto all sides.

3 Cut out your paper pattern.

4 Fold your lining fabric in half and pin the pattern on.

5 Cut around the pattern, cutting through two thicknesses of fabric.

6 Sew the two pieces together as you did for the knitted pieces. Some bags will have their corners turned in to form a base. Do the same for the lining.

The instructions for making the simple lining can be adapted for shaped bags, such as the Retro Revamp bag (pages 98–99). The lining retains the shape of the bag and prevents it from stretching.

A SIMPLE LINING FOR A SHAPED BAG

This is a lining for a bag with only two pieces, a back and front, but each is shaped rather than just a straight rectangle or square. You will need the same materials as given for the simple lining.
Work steps 1 and 2 as given for simple lining.

3 Lay the front on the paper in the rectangle matching the base and top edge. Carefully draw around the shaping. Remove the front and use a ruler to straighten the lines.

4 Add a seam allowance of ⅞in (1.5cm) onto all sides.

Continue as given for simple lining from step 3.

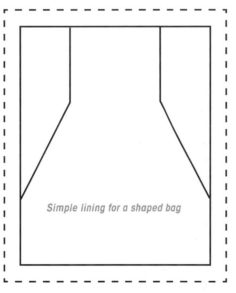

Simple lining for a shaped bag

A LINING FOR A BAG WITH A FLAT BASE

This type of lining requires a bit more measuring and drawing, but is well worth the extra effort. The flat base means that your bag will stand properly and the base will also hold out the gussets to give the bag depth. The When the Cows Come Home tote bag (pages 60–63) has a flat base, as does the Frills and Spills bag (pages 64–66). If you look at the knitted pieces, you will see that they look as though they have two squares cut out on each side seam at the bottom edge. Joining the two sides of this missing square will form the corner of the bag and therefore the gusset and base.

You will need the same materials as given for the simple lining.

1 Press your knitted pieces to size, making sure the edges are straight and corners square. The back and front should be the same size.

2 Measure the length and width of the front. Draw a square or rectangle onto the paper using these measurements. Measure the two sides of the missing square. Draw this onto your pattern. Add a seam allowance of ⅞in (1.5cm) onto all sides. Work steps 3, 4 and 5 as for simple lining above.

6 Sew the two pieces together as for the knitted pieces, forming the corners as instructed.

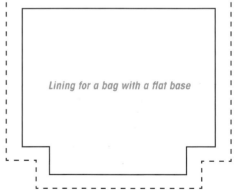

Lining for a bag with a flat base

The Off the Cuff bag (pages 32–35) has a flat base but also has shaped edges. Work step 1 as above.

2 Measure the length and width of the front. Draw a square or rectangle onto the paper using these measurements.

3 Lay the front on the paper in the rectangle matching the long side and the top edge. Carefully draw up each shaped edge. Add a seam allowance of ⅞in (1.5cm) onto all sides Work steps 3 to 6 as given for the simple lining.

For structured bags, such as the In The Pink bag (page 67), follow the instructions for making a flat base to give the bag strength and depth, allowing it to stand properly.

3 Lay the front on the paper in the rectangle matching the long side and side edges. Carefully draw around the curved edge.

4 Add a seam allowance of ⅝in (1.5cm) onto all sides.

5 Cut out your paper pattern.

6 Repeat step 2 for each of the other pieces, adding seam allowances.

7 Fold your lining fabric in half, pin the pattern on and cut around each pattern piece, cutting through two thicknesses of fabric.

8 Use the pattern for the front to cut out two pieces of heavy-weight interfacing. If using iron-on interfacing, omit the seam allowances.

9 Iron or sew on the interfacing to the front and back.

10 Make up the lining as you did for the knitted pieces.

MAKING A FLAT BASE

The base is a removable insert of thick card. I usually use greyboard, which is sold in art and craft shops for bookbinding. It is extremely strong and doesn't bend. Alternatively, you could use heavy-weight sew-in interfacing or plastic canvas. You can also use this without a lining.

YOU WILL NEED
the same materials as given for the simple lining
greyboard/thick card
craft knife

1 Measure the width and depth of your bag after it has been made up. If you have already drawn a pattern for the lining, you could measure this, omitting seam allowances.

2 Draw a rectangle onto the greyboard using these measurements. Cut out carefully using the craft knife.

3 To cover the greyboard with fabric, draw around it onto the paper. As the board is quite thick, you need to include a bit extra when you draw on the seam allowance. Add a seam allowance of ¾in (2cm) onto the two short sides and one long side.

4 Cut out your paper pattern.

5 Fold your lining fabric in half, pin the pattern on with the long side without a seam allowance to the fold in the fabric.

6 Cut around the pattern, cutting through two thicknesses of fabric.

7 Sew the long seam and one short seam, using a seam allowance of ⅝in (1.5cm).

8 Insert the greyboard. Fold the extra fabric at the open edge to the inside and slipstitch the edges closed.

9 Push into the bag and secure with a few stitches in each corner.

MAKING A STIFFENED LINING

You will need a stiffened lining to make the Bowled Over bag (pages 56–59). This has more than a front and a back; it has zip panels as well as a separate base and side panels. It also relies on the lining to add stiffness. Without it, the shape would collapse. To stiffen the lining, use a heavy-weight interfacing, either sew-in or iron-on if your lining can withstand a high iron temperature.

YOU WILL NEED
the same materials as given for the simple lining
heavy-weight interfacing

1 Press all the knitted pieces, making sure the edges are straight and the corners square. Pieces that you made two of should be the same size.

2 Measure the length and width of the front. Draw a rectangle onto the paper using these measurements.

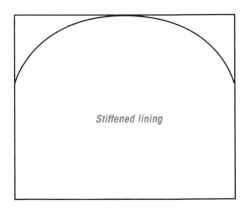

Stiffened lining

FULLED BAGS

Most fulled bags will not need lining; the fabric will have thickened and any strands from intarsia or Fair Isle will have been merged into the fabric. If you want to line your bag, it will have been made up before fulling, so you can't draw around the pieces. So you should lay the bag out flat, squashing out the side pieces. Measure the total width and the length of the front. Use these measurements to make the pattern piece, as given for the simple lining.

adding zips

Zips are a great way to close long or curved edges that might otherwise gape. I have used zips to fasten the Look, no Hands! and Hands-Free bags (pages 50–55), the Bowled Over bag (pages 56–59), and the Falling Leaves bag (pages 42–45). The Daisy Days purse (pages 90–92) also has a zip closure.

BUYING ZIPS

Zips can have nylon or metal teeth. The metal ones tend to be chunkier and heavier than the nylon ones, so use these for thicker fabrics, like the Bowled Over bag. For this bag, I used two metal zips specifically made for denim jeans. Nylon zips are available in a wider range of colours and are more flexible than metal ones. This makes them more suitable for curved edges, like on the Look, No Hands! bag and Hands-Free handbag, and the Falling Leaves bag.

Zips are available in standard lengths; if you can't find one to fit exactly then buy one longer than you need. I struggled to find a zip small enough for the daisy purse, so bought a 6in (15cm) zip. You can easily shorten zips by working some strong binding stitches around the zip teeth at the required length. This holds the teeth together and you can then trim away the excess length.

Match the colour of your zip to the yarn you have used. If you can't find an exact match, go for a shade darker. Alternatively, you could make the zip part of the bag's design; choose a brightly coloured chunky zip and add matching beads to the pull.

SEWING IN THE ZIP

Always hand-sew your zip into the bag; never use a sewing machine, as it will stretch the knitted fabric. Measure the opening and the zip carefully and make sure they are both the same size. Never stretch the knitting to fit a too-long zip or gather it to fit a too-short zip. The zip will never lie correctly and will be difficult to open and close.

1 Divide the knitted zip edging, panel or top edge of the bag into quarters and mark with pins. Do the same with the zip.
2 Carefully pin one side of the zip into place, matching the pin markers, and matching the edge of the knitted fabric to the edge of the teeth.
3 Using a contrasting thread, tack the zip into place.
Work steps 1 to 3 again for the other side of the bag and the zip.

Using a strong sewing thread and a sharp needle, begin sewing the zip into the bag, using a small neat backstitch. Sew down any fabric zip ends that may interfere with the opening.

OTHER FASTENINGS
Buttons

The easiest way to close a bag is to add a button loop with a button. Buttons are also a great way to embellish your bag at the same time. Choose a large feature button, as on the Buttons and Bows bag (pages 82–85) or a jeans button on denim yarn. I used metal buttons for the Look, No Hands! bag (pages 50–53) to go with the military khaki, but hot pink ones for the Hands-Free handbag version (pages 54–55). The diamanté button on the In a Flap bag (pages 26–27) adds an unexpected twist, and the Off the Cuff bag (pages 32–35) has suit buttons to carry on that theme. There are so many styles available that it is easy to match colour, material or theme.

Button loops

You can make a loop out of ribbon, as I've done for the Off the Cuff bag (pages 32–35), use braid or cord, or make a short twisted cord from the yarn used for the bag. Knit a cord such as the one used on the Coming Up Roses bag (page 25). A loop covered with buttonhole stitch has been used on the Patching It Up bag (pages 28–31).

To make this loop, mark the position of your button loop on the back of the bag. Pin the button into place on the front. Thread a blunt needle with your yarn and secure it to the WS of the back just below the top edge to match the position of the button. Make a loop the required size by working loosely around the button placed on the front, then take the yarn to the back and secure. Take the needle back to the beginning again to make a double loop. Work buttonhole stitch (page 120) over the loop, covering it from end to end.

Brooches and beads

Use a brooch instead of a button. Look out for old ones that may have lost their pins and recycle them onto your bag. A large bead would also make a great fastening; how about a handmade glass bead or a carved wooden one?

handles

You can change the handles on any of the projects in this book. Most of them have knitted handles; some have bought ready-made ones. You might want to make a handbag into a shoulder bag, or vice versa. You may have knitted your bag in a different yarn or colour and now need a more elegant handle or a lighter one. Lengths will vary with people's taste; you may like a short shoulder strap while someone else likes long straps. That's why I always suggest trying your bag on to check the length of straps or handles.

KNITTED HANDLES

These are easy to alter. You can knit extra length for a strap, knit fewer stitches for a thinner, lighter handle, or thread cord or tape through to strengthen them. More detailed instructions on how to work the variations below can be found by following the individual bag references.

Garter-stitch handles

I've used these on the Patching it Up bag (pages 28–31) and the Daisy Days bag (pages 90–92); they are a really simple way of adding a different handle. You need to cast on enough stitches for the length of handle that you want; work this out from the gauge on the ball band for your chosen yarn. Knit three or four rows and bind off. Knitting the handle widthways rather than lengthwise stops the garter stitch from stretching too much. If you want to use garter stitch for a strap, cast on stitches for the width you want and knit every row until it is long enough. Remember that garter stitch will stretch, so pull it out when you measure it. It is better to knit it shorter than you need.

Stockinette-stitch handles

These are more stable than garter-stitch handles; they don't stretch as much. Double-thickness ones are better to use on larger bags or those with more structure. I've used them for the Frills and Flounces bags (pages 64–67). Work them widthwise for handbags. Use the gauge on the ball band for your chosen yarn to work out the number of stitches to cast on. Knit it twice the finished

width, fold in half and slipstitch the cast-on edge to the bound-off edge. Press firmly so it lies flat. For the In the Pink frilly bag (page 67) and on the Simply Chic bags (pages 20–27) I used a single thickness for the handle. It rolls up to make a tube and is ideal for bags that use a delicate yarn. For longer handles or straps, such as those on the Instant Messenger bag (pages 86–89) and on the Falling Leaves bag (pages 42–45), cast on the required width and work in stockinette stitch. Make two the same and sew together down each side. This means you can also thread tape or webbing through the handle strengthen it.

Tubular knitted cord handles

These are used on several projects including the Square Dance bag (pages 68–71), the Buttons and Bows bag (pages 82–85) and the Bowled Over bag (pages 56–59) – see page 121 for instructions. I always add a flat end to these handles to make them easier to sew on. They are tubes of knitting worked on double-pointed needles. Thread a thick piping cord through them for strength and to round out the tube. When you do this, you will notice a small ladder running up the tube. I close this by using a crochet hook to 'knit up' the loose strands; this also tightens the knitting around the cord.

Twisted cord handles

Twisted cords (see page 121) are ideal for small items, such as the Quick Draw drawstring bags (pages 72–77). The more strands you use, the thicker the cord will be, so use four, five or six to make a strap.

BOUGHT HANDLES

Several of the bags have been finished with a bought ready-made handle. Bought handles are available in a wide range of styles and materials, and are a quick and easy way to alter the look of a bag.

D-shape or arched handles

Many arched handles have slits at the ends to work stitches through. The Off the Cuff bag (pages 32–35) features a pair of clear plastic arched handles, which are attached using tabs of ribbon. They could just as easily be sewn on, using yarn and whipstitch. These types of handles could also have metal rings at the ends for attaching to the bag.

Rings

The Fantastic Flowers bag (pages 78–81) is knitted extra-long to encase the bamboo rings. To add them to a bag with a straight top, knit two 5in (12.5cm) lengths of garter stitch ten stitches wide, sew one end of each centrally onto the back and front of the bag, thread through the rings, and sew down the other end.

Other shapes

You can also buy square and oval handles, in plastic, bamboo or wood, in faux tortoiseshell or in bright colours and patterns.

Metal frames

The Classic Colours Fair Isle bag (pages 94–97) is sewn into an elaborate frame, which has loops for a chain handle. Alternatively, you could make a twisted cord, as I did. Frames are available in many widths; look at the internal width rather than the width of the whole frame, as this is the part you sew your knitted fabric into. The frame has a row of holes around its edge for sewing through. Plainer frames, frames with integral handles and ones with ornate fastenings in silver or gold will give an old-fashioned look to your bag, while more modern styles in dark nickel or copper are a fantastic way to add a professional finish to your bag.

Beaded handles

Crystal beads would add glamour to an evening bag, while wooden beads would complement the natural look of linen or hemp. To make your own, cut two lengths of craft wire to the required measurement. Coil one end up to stop the beads falling off. Thread your beads on the other end. Coil this end up to secure the beads. Attach to bag with yarn, sewing through the coils, or thin ribbon threaded through the coils.

Fabric handles

There is a wide range of ribbons, braids, upholstery trimmings and tapes available in different materials and widths. Use ribbons for smaller bags, such as the Always the Bridesmaid bag (page 24) and stronger webbings or tapes for more robust bags such as the When the Cows Come Home bag (pages 60–63). Look out for unusual designs of upholstery trims – some have fringes or bullions, which would make fun handles.

embellishments

There are many ways to add a final embellishment to your work. Simple embroidery stitches will add an individual touch to your knitted bag. Use embroidery as a small detail on a pocket or flap, or cover the bag with a more complex pattern. Cords, tassels and pompoms are also quick and easy ways to work your own design.

KNIT PERFECT

Use embroidery threads, tapestry wools or knitting yarn; it should be the same or slightly thicker than the knitted yarn. Check that the threads are colourfast and will not shrink when washed. Work an embroidered sample and wash it if you are not certain.

Use a large-eyed blunt tapestry needle. Work the embroidery stitches loosely; don't pull too tightly or the knitted fabric will pucker. To begin the embroidery, weave the end of the thread through a few knitted stitches on the back of the fabric, working back through the thread to secure it; if you start with a knot, it may come undone during wear.

EMBROIDERY

I've used backstitch to add the stems and spirals on the Fantastic Flowers bag (pages 78–81), and lazy daisy stitch on the tiny Daisy Days purse (pages 90–92). Swiss darning is a great way to add colour and pattern to plain stockinette stitch, or to work Fair Isle motifs; this is the method I used for the Retro Revamp bag (pages 98–99) instead of knitting the pattern in Fair Isle.

BACKSTITCH

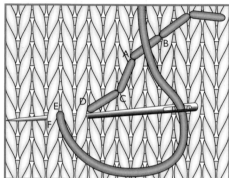

Backstitch forms a continuous line that can be used for outlining, for stems or for adding details. To begin, bring the needle up at A. In one movement, take the needle down at B and up at C. Take it down at A and up at D, down at C and up at E, down at D and up at F.

SWISS DARNING

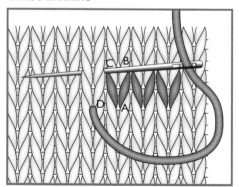

This stitch (also known as duplicate stitch) looks as though it has been knitted into the fabric; it follows the line of the yarn for the knit stitch on the right side of stockinette stitch. It is used to embroider small areas of colour such as a motif that would be tedious to knit, or you can use it to cover up any colours that you don't like in a stripe pattern. Use the same thickness of yarn used for the knitting. Take care to insert the needle between the strands and not to split the knitted

LAZY DAISY STITCH

This stitch is formed from individual chain stitches worked around a centre to create the petals of a flower. The loops are fastened with a small stitch. Bring the needle out at A. In one movement, push the needle down in the same place and bring it out at B, looping the thread under the needle tip. Take the needle back down at B, working over the loop, and bring it up at A for the next stitch.

stitches. The stitches will appear slightly raised on the surface of the knitting.

Horizontal stitches

Work from right to left, bringing the needle out at the base of the stitch (A). In one movement, take the thread around the top of the stitch by taking the needle down at B and up at C. In one movement, take the needle down at the base of the stitch (A) and up at the base of the next stitch (D). Continue across the row.

Vertical stitches

Work from bottom to top, bringing the needle out at the base of the stitch (A). Take the thread around the top of the stitch (B and C) and back down at the base (A). This time, bring the needle up at the base of the stitch above and continue up the line of knitted stitches.

BUTTONHOLE STITCH

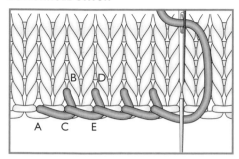

You can use this as a decorative edging along a knitted item, or to reinforce a button loop. Often used to neaten raw edges, this stitch can be worked from left to right or from right to left. Bring the needle out at A. In one movement, take it down at B and back up at C, looping the thread under the needle tip. The next stitch is worked to the right, down at D and up at E. The horizontal threads should lie on the edge of the fabric.

TWISTED CORD

Strands of yarn twisted together will form a cord. The more strands you use, the thicker the cord will be. Cut lengths of yarn three times the finished length required and tie them together with a knot at each end. Hook one end over a doorknob or hook and, holding the other knotted end, stand back so that the strands are taut. Insert a pencil into the end and wind it to twist the strands. Keep the strands taut as you wind, twisting until the cord starts to fold up and twist around itself. Keeping the cord taut, remove the end from the doorknob and bring both knotted ends together. The cord will twist around itself. Ask someone to hold the middle or hang a weight from a hook on the middle of the cord to hold it taut as it twists. Small tassels can be made at either end by knotting the strands, cutting the looped end and then untying the knots from the other end. A textured cord is made by combining different yarns or colours.

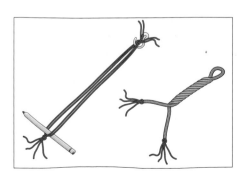

TUBULAR KNITTED CORD

This long tube, sometimes called I-cord, is knitted on two double-pointed needles. Cast on four stitches and knit one row. Do not turn the work but instead push the stitches to the other end of the needle. Swap the right-hand needle with the left-hand needle, pull up the yarn and knit the four stitches again. Repeat for every row. By pulling the yarn up at the end of the row, the edges of the knitting are pulled together and a tube if formed. Cast on three stitches for a finer cord, and five stitches for a thicker one. Piping cord can be threaded through the knitted cord to make bag handles more resilient.

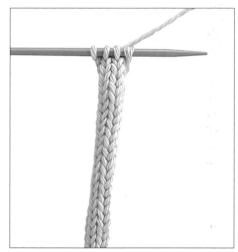

OTHER EMBELLISHMENTS

Pompom

These are great for finishing off the ends of a cord or drawstring. You could make several and sew them in a line around the top of a bag for a fluffy trim.

Cut two circles out of stiff cardboard. They should be the same diameter that you require for the finished pompom. Cut out a hole in the centre of each one half of this size. Cut a wedge shape out of the circles. Place them together and begin winding yarn around them until the hole in the centre is filled. Carefully cut through the loops all the way around, being careful not to let any yarn strands escape. Pull a length of yarn between the two pieces of cardboard, knot the two ends together and pull tightly around the centre of the pompom. Secure with a tight knot. Pull out the cardboard circles. Fluff up the pompom, trimming any uneven ends, but leave the two yarn ends for sewing onto your knitted item.

Braided cord

Cut a number (a multiple of three) of strands of yarn twice the length of your finished braid. Tie the ends together at one end. Divide the strands into three bunches. Make the braided cord by passing the right-hand bunch over the centre bunch, and then under the left-hand bunch. Pass the right-hand bunch over the centre bunch, then under the left-hand bunch, tightening the weaving as you work. Repeat this until the cord is the right length. Tie a small knot into the end to prevent the plaited cord unravelling, and trim the ends into a neat tassel.

Tassels

Wrap the yarn loosely around a piece of card the required length of the tassel. Thread a long length of yarn under the strands at the top, fold in half and tie in tight knot, leaving two long ends. Cut the wrapped strands at the bottom and remove the cardboard. Thread one long end on to a tapestry needle, insert it through the top of the tassel and bring out 1in (2.5cm) below. Wrap the yarn several times around the tassel. Pass the needle through the middle of the wrapped strands to secure the long end, then insert the needle again up through the top of the tassel. Use the long ends to sew in place. Trim the bottom of the tassel neatly to make a straight edge.

troubleshooting

Even the most accomplished knitters make mistakes and come up against challenges, so don't be disheartened if you go wrong occasionally. These techniques show you the easy way to rectify your mistakes and find the way forward.

DROPPED STITCHES

A dropped stitch is a stitch that has fallen off your needle and has unravelled down a few rows, creating a ladder. The sooner you spot that you have dropped a stitch, the easier it is to rectify the mistake. Get into the habit of checking your knitting every few rows.

Knit stitch dropped one row below

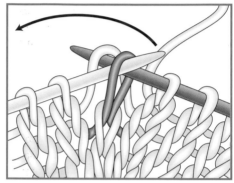

Insert the right needle through the front of the dropped stitch and then pick up the strand of yarn behind it. With the tip of the left needle, pass the stitch over the strand and off the needle.

Purl stitch dropped one row below

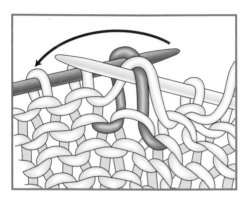

Insert the right needle through the back of the dropped stitch and then pick up the yarn strand in front of it. With the left needle, pass the stitch over the strand and off the needle.

Stitch dropped several rows below

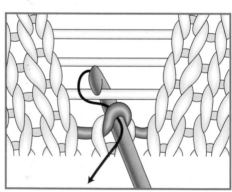

Find the dropped stitch – it will be a loop at the base of a ladder of strands of yarn. Insert a crochet hook through the front of the loop of the dropped stitch, catch the yarn strand immediately above it and pull through the stitch. Repeat for all the strands of the ladder until you reach the top. Slip the stitch back onto the left-hand needle.

To pick up a dropped purl stitch, work as given for a knit stitch but turn your work around so that you are working on the wrong side of the fabric. If more than one stitch has been dropped, slip the others on to a safety pin to stop them running any further, while you pick them up one by one. If you drop a stitch and do not notice it until a lot of knitting later, the ladder will have closed up at the top and there will be no strands of yarn to pick up with the crochet hook. Unfortunately, the only solution is to unravel your work back to the dropped stitch. If you try to pick it up by stealing yarn from the neighbouring stitches, it will create an area of tightened stitches and spoil your knitting.

UNRAVELLING ONE ROW

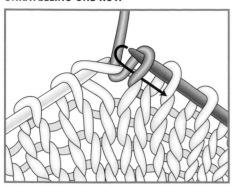

If you have made an error in the stitches that you have just worked on the right needle, for example in a stitch pattern or knitting when you should have purled, there is no need to take the work off the needle to unravel back to that point. You can just unravel, stitch by stitch, back to the error. Insert the left needle into the stitch below from the front, drop the stitch off the right needle and pull the yarn. Repeat this for each stitch back to the error. Work in the same way for purl stitches.

UNRAVELLING SEVERAL ROWS

If you have to unravel several rows, slip the needles out of the stitches carefully, gather the work up into one hand and unravel each row to the row above the error. Do not be tempted to lay the work out flat to do this, as you are more likely to pull the stitches roughly, which often results in you pulling out more than you want. Replace the stitches on to the needle and then unravel the last row carefully as given above. By doing this you have more control over the final row and are less likely to drop or miss any stitches. If you find that after unravelling, your needle is facing the wrong way, slip the stitches purlwise back onto another needle so that you are ready to knit. If you have a suitably sized double-pointed or circular needle, you can use this and then be able to work straight off either end of it.

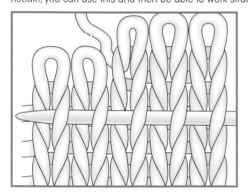

If you are using a slippery yarn or one that will not unravel easily, such as a hairy yarn, or if you are nervous about dropping stitches during unravelling, you can pick up stitches in the row below the error and then unravel knowing the stitches are safe on a needle. Take a spare needle that is smaller than that used for the knitting and weave it through the first loop and over the second loop of each stitch on the row below the mistake. Then pull the work back to these stitches. Make sure you put aside the smaller needle and pick up the correct size to continue knitting.

If you are working a cable or stitch pattern, you should pick the nearest row to the error without too much patterning and where you can see the stitches clearly.

RUNNING OUT OF YARN

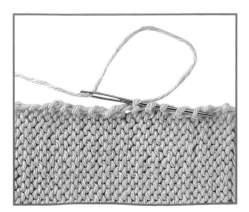

When you run out of yarn and need to start a new ball or need to change to another colour, always start it at the beginning of a row or at a seam edge where the ends can be woven in neatly.

Simply drop the old yarn, wrap the new yarn around the needle and work a few stitches. Tie the two ends securely together at the beginning of the row so neither one will work its way free and unravel your stitches. When you have finished the piece, undo the knot and weave one end up the edge for a couple of inches, and then double back

SPLIT YARN

You can easily split a strand of yarn if you are working fast, or, if you are using a yarn mix of several strands, it is easy to miss working through one of the strands. You should go back and rework it correctly, since any split like this will show up on your fabric. Use one of the unravelling methods described to go back to the split stitch.

INCOMPLETE STITCHES

These occur where you have wrapped the yarn around the needle but it has not been pulled through the old stitch to form a new stitch. The yarn strand will be on the needle next to the unworked stitch. Work the stitch properly with the yarn strand as given for dropped stitches.

CABLES

If you have twisted a cable the wrong way, and you have spotted it within a few rows, unravel the cable stitches only and reknit by using the long loops of yarn released by unravelling. If the error is a long way down the piece and the cable has been twisted again after the error, you will have to unravel the work and reknit all of it.

SNAGGED STITCHES

If you snag a stitch, a loop of yarn is pulled out, drawing up tightly several stitches around it. Using a tapestry needle, ease the extra yarn back through the distorted stitches, one by one, starting with the stitch closest to the snag and yarn loop.

over a few stitches to secure the end. Make sure you haven't pulled it too tightly and distorted the edge. Weave the other end down the edge using the same method.

If you are coming to the end of a ball, to see if you have enough yarn to work one more row, lay the knitting flat and measure the yarn four times across the width. This will be sufficient to work one row of stockinette stitch; textured and cabled fabric will need more yarn. When in doubt, join in a new ball of yarn to avoid running out of yarn halfway through and having to unravel stitches.

yarns used

Below are listed the specific yarns that were used for the projects in this book, should you wish to recreate them exactly as we have. Yarn companies frequently discontinue colours or yarns, and replace them with new yarns. Therefore, you may find that some of the yarns or colours below are no longer available. However, by referring to the yarn descriptions on the project pages, you should have no trouble finding a substitute.

SUBSTITUTING YARNS

To work out how much replacement yarn you need, just follow these simple steps. Use it for each colour or yarn used in the project.
1 The number of balls of the recommended yarn x the number of yards/metres per ball = A
2 The number of yards/metres per ball of the replacement yarn = B
3 A ÷ B = number of balls of replacement yarn.

Page 20 Simply Chic Bags
Just Fur You
2 x 1¾oz (50g) balls of Sirdar Foxy (100% polyester – 44yd/40m per ball) in colour 435
All the Trimmings
A 1 x 1¾oz (50g) ball of Sirdar Silky Look DK (93% acrylic/7% nylon – 147yd/135m per ball) in colour 964
B 1 x 1¾oz (50g) ball of Louisa Harding Fauve (100% nylon – 127yd/116m per ball) in colour 12
Always the Bridesmaid
A 1 x 1¾oz (50g) ball of Rowan Wool Cotton (50% wool/50% cotton – 123yd/113m per ball) in colour 900
B 1 x ⅞oz (25g) ball of GGH Velour (100% nylon – 63yd/58m per ball) in colour 01
C 1 x 1¾oz (50g) ball of GGH Domino (44% cotton/43% acrylic/13% polyester – 136yd/125m per ball) in colour 18
D 1 x 1¾oz (50g) ball of Jaeger Odessa DK (65% mohair/31% acrylic/4% polyester metal – 174yd/190m per ball) in colour 160
Coming Up Roses
A 2 x 1¾oz (50g) balls of Rowan All Seasons Cotton (60% cotton/40% acrylic – 98yd/90m per ball) in colour 214
B 1 x 1¾oz (50g) ball of Rowan Summer Tweed (70% silk/30% cotton – 118yd/108m per ball) in colour 522
In a Flap
1 x 3½oz (100g) ball of Rowan Yorkshire Tweed Aran (100% wool – 175yd/160m per ball) in colour 411
1 x ⅞oz (25g) ball of Rowan Kidsilk Haze (70% kid mohair/30% silk – 229yd/210m per ball) in colour 582

Page 28 Patching It Up
A 1 x 1¾oz (50g) ball of Jaeger Trinity DK (40% silk/35% cotton/25% polyamide – 218yd/200m per ball) in colour 432
B 1 x ⅞oz (25g) ball of Rowan Kidsilk Haze (70% kid mohair/30% silk – 229yd/210m per ball) in colour 606
C 1 x 1¾oz (50g) ball of Jaeger Aqua cotton (100% cotton – 115yd/106m per ball) in colour 322
D 1 x 1¾oz (50g) ball of Debbie Bliss cotton angora (80% cotton/20% angora – 98yd/90m per ball) in colour 15509
E 2 x 1¾oz (50g) balls of Debbie Bliss alpaca silk DK (80% alpaca/20% silk – 114yd/105m per ball) in colour 26006

Page 32 Off the Cuff
A 2 x 1¾oz (50g) balls of Rowan Cashsoft DK (57% merino wool/33% microfibre/10% cashmere – 142yd/130m per ball) in colour 518
B 2 x ⅞oz (25g) balls of Twilley's Goldfingering (80% viscose/20% metallized polyester – 218yd/200m per ball) in colour WG5
Rose Corsage
Oddments of dark red (A) and dark green (B) light-weight (DK) wool yarn

Page 36 Classy Convertibles
Get Back Backpack
4 x 1¾oz (50g) balls of Noro Blossom (40% wool/30% kid mohair/20% silk/10% nylon – 95yd/87m per hank) in colour 17
Secret Life Shoulder Bag
A 4 x 1¾oz (50g) balls of Debbie Bliss cashmerino astrakhan (60% wool/30% microfibre/10% cashmere – 76yd/70m per ball) in colour 004
B 3 x 1¾oz (50g) balls of Jaeger Matchmaker DK (100% wool – 131yd/120m per ball) in colour 728

Page 42 Falling Leaves
A 2 x 1¾oz (50g) balls of Rowan Scottish Tweed DK (100% wool – 123yd/113m per ball) in colour 15
B 6 x 8m skeins of DMC Tapestry Wool (100% wool) in colours 7922, 7947, 7740, 7125, 7946, 7214

Page 46 Lacy Lovelies
Summertime Sweetie
1 x 3½oz (100g) ball of Sirdar Pure Cotton 4ply (100% cotton – 370yd/338m per ball) in colour 21
Pretty in Purple
3 x ⅞oz (25g) balls of Rowan Scottish tweed 4ply (100% wool – 120yd/110m per ball) in colour 16

Page 50 Belt Up Bags
Look, No Hands!
3 x 1¾oz (50g) balls of Jaeger Roma (63% viscose/22% nylon/15% angora – 137yd/125m per ball) in colour 6
Hands-Free Handbag
3 x 1¾oz (50g) balls of Debbie Bliss alpaca silk DK (80% alpaca/20% silk – 114yd/105m per ball) in colour 006

Page 56 Bowled Over
A 4 x 1¾oz (50g) balls of Debbie Bliss Cotton

Denim Aran (100% cotton – 74yd/68m per ball) in colour 502

B 1 x 1¾oz (50g) ball of Jaeger Aqua (100% mercerized cotton – 115yd/106m per ball) in colour 332

Page 60 When the Cows Come Home

3 x 1¾oz (50g) balls of Debbie Bliss Cashmerino Astrakhan (60% wool/30% microfibre/10% cashmere – 76yd/70m per ball) in each of colour 03 (A) and colour 01 (B)

Page 64 Frills and Flounces
Frills and Spills

A 2 x 1¾oz (50g) balls of Rowan All Seasons Cotton DK (60% cotton/40% acrylic – 98yd/905m per ball) in colour 175

B 2 x 1¾oz (50g) balls of Rowan Handknit Cotton DK (100% cotton – 93yd/85m per ball) in colour 215

In the Pink

2 x 1¾oz (50g) balls of Jaeger Luxury Tweed DK (65% merino lambswool/35% alpaca – 197yd/180m per ball) in colour 827

Page 68 Square Dance

5 x 1¾oz (50g) balls of Noro Kureyon (100% wool – 109yd/100m per ball) in colour 170

Page 72 Quick Draw
Snow Queen

A 1 x 1¾oz (50g) ball of Sirdar Funky Fur (100% polyester – 98yd/90m per ball) in colour 512

B 1 x 1¾oz (50g) ball of Sirdar Luxury Soft Cotton DK (100% cotton – 104yd/95m per ball) in colour 652

C 1 x 1¾oz (50g) ball of Sirdar Snuggly Bubbly DK (100% nylon – 140yd/128m per ball) in colour 190

D 1 x 1¾oz (50g) ball of Sirdar Silky Look DK (93% acrylic/7% nylon – 147yd/135m per ball) in colour 911

Springtime Shimmer

A 1 x 1¾oz (50g) ball of Sirdar Funky Fur (100% polyester – 98yd/90m per ball) in colour 513

B 1 x 1¾oz (50g) ball of Rowan Soft Baby DK (50% wool/30% polyamide/20% cotton – 164yd/150m per ball) in colour 07

C 1 x 1¾oz (50g) ball of Sirdar Dune DK (100% nylon – 109yd/100m per ball) in colour 453

D 1 x 1¾oz (50g) ball of Sirdar Snuggly Chatterbox DK (58% acrylic/42% nylon – 137yd/125m per ball) in colour 339

Summer Shades

A 1 x ⅞oz (25g) ball of GGH soft kid (70% kid mohair/25% nylon/5% wool – 150yd/137m per ball) in colour 55

B 1 x 1¾oz (50g) ball of Jaeger Aqua Cotton DK (100% cotton – 115yd/106m per ball) in colour 309

C 1 x 1¾oz (50g) ball of Debbie Bliss Cashmerino Astrakhan (60% wool/30% microfibre/10% cashmere – 76yd/70m per ball) in colour 16

D 1 x 1¾oz (50g) ball of Patons Coral DK (61% cotton/39% acrylic – 137yd/125m per ball) in colour 1015

Fall Fantastic

A 1 x 1¾oz (50g) ball of Sirdar Boa (100% polyester – 102yd/93m per ball) in colour 33

B 1 x 1¾oz (50g) ball of Artesano Alpaca Inca Cloud (100% alpaca – 131yd/120m per ball) in colour 71

C 1 x 1¾oz (50g) ball of Jaeger Aqua Cotton DK (100% cotton – 115yd/106m per ball) in colour 321 and 1 x 3½oz (100g) ball of South West Trading Melody (65% rayon/35% nylon – 400yd/366m per ball) in colour 516

D 1 x 1¾oz (50g) ball of Rowan Felted Tweed DK (50% wool/25% alpaca/25% viscose – 191yd/175m per ball) in colour 155 and 1 x ⅞oz (25g) ball of Rowan Lurex Shimmer (80% viscose/20% polyester – 104yd/95m per ball) in colour 331

Heart On Your Sleeve

A 1 x 1¾oz (50g) ball of GGH Aldente (63% wool/37% nylon – 120yd/110m per ball) in colour 2

B 1 x ⅞oz (25g) ball of GGH Soft Kid (70% kid mohair/25% nylon/5% wool – 104yd/95m per ball) in colour 32

Page 78 Fantastic Flowers

A 3 x 1¾oz (50g) balls of Rowan Handknit Cotton DK (100% cotton – 93yd/85m per ball) in colour 313

B 1 x 1¾oz (50g) ball of Rowan Handknit Cotton DK (100% cotton – 93yd/85m per ball) in colour 319

C 1 x 1¾oz (50g) ball of Rowan Handknit Cotton DK (100% cotton – 93yd/85m per ball) in colour 219

Page 82 Buttons and Bows

3 x 1¾oz (50g) balls of Jaeger Extra Fine Merino DK (100% wool – 137yd/125m per ball) in colour 937

Page 86 Instant Messenger

7 x 1¾oz (50g) balls of Rowan Summer Tweed (70% silk/30% cotton – 118yd/108m per ball) in colour 529

Page 90 Posy Purses
Daisy Days

A 1 x 1¾oz (50g) ball of Rowan Cotton Glace (100% cotton – 125yd/115m per ball) in colour 814

B 1 x 1¾oz (50g) ball of Rowan Cotton Glace (100% cotton – 125yd/115m per ball) in colour 726

Rose Petal Purse

A 1 x 1¾oz (50g) ball of Debbie Bliss Pure Silk (100% silk – 136yd/125m per ball) in colour 27005

B 1 x 1¾oz (50g) ball of Debbie Bliss Pure Silk (100% silk – 136yd/125m per ball) in colour 27004

Page 94 Fabulous Fair Isle
Classic Colours

A 1 x 1¾oz (50g) ball of Patons Spritz Aran (76% acrylic/24% metallic fibres – 126yd/115m per ball) in colour 002

B 1 x 1¾oz (50g) ball of Jaeger Aqua Cotton DK (100% cotton – 115yd/106m per ball) in colour 320

C 1 x 1¾oz (50g) ball of Sirdar Luxury Soft Cotton DK (100% cotton – 104yd/95m per ball) in colour 650

D 1 x 1¾oz (50g) ball of RCY Luxury Cotton DK (50% cotton/45% viscose/5% silk – 104yd/95m per ball) in colour 253

E 1 x 1¾oz (50g) ball of RCY Luxury Cotton DK (50% cotton/45% viscose/5% silk – 104yd/95m per ball) in colour 255

Retro Revamp

A 1 x ⅞oz (25g) ball of Twilley's Goldfingering (80% viscose/20% metallized polyester – 218yd/200m per ball) in colour WG2

B 1 x 1¾oz (50g) ball of Rowan Handknit Cotton DK (100% cotton – 93yd/85m per ball) in colour 215

C 1 x 1¾oz (50g) ball of Rowan Summer Tweed (70% silk/30% cotton -- 118yd/108m per ball) in colour 503

D 1 x 1¾oz (50g) ball of Rowan Cotton Glace (100% cotton – 125yd/115m per ball) in colour 820

E 1 x 1¾oz (50g) ball of Debbie Bliss Cotton DK (100% cotton – 92yd/84m per ball) in colour 042

suppliers

Contact the manufacturers for your local stockist or go to their websites for stockist and mail order information.

Debbie Bliss
www.debbieblissonline.com
(USA) Knitting Fever Inc.
315 Bayview Avenue, Amityville, NY 11701
Tel: 001 516 5463600
e-mail: knittingfever@knittingfever.com
www.knittingfever.com
(UK) Designer Yarns Ltd
Units 8–10 Newbridge Industrial Estate, Pitt Street,
Keighley, West Yorkshire, BD21 4PQ
Tel: 01535 664222
www.designeryarns.uk.com
(AUS) Prestige Yarns Pty Ltd
PO Box 39, Bulli, NSW 2516
Tel: 02 4285 6669
e-mail: info@prestigeyarns.com
www.prestigeyarns.com

DMC
(USA) The DMC Corporation
10 Port Kearney, South Kearney, NJ, 070732
Tel: 973 589 0606
www.dmc-usa.com
(UK) DMC Creative World Ltd
Pullman Road, Wigston, Leicester, LE18 2DY
Tel: 0116 281 1040
www.dmc.com
(AUS) For a list of stockists go to their website at
www.dmc.com

GGH
www.ggh-garn.de
(USA) Muench Yarns Inc
1323 Scott Street, Petaluma, CA 94954-1135
Tel: (800) 733-9276
e-mail: info@muenchyarns.com
www.muenchyarns.com
(UK) Designer Yarns Ltd
Units 8–10 Newbridge Industrial Estate, Pitt Street,
Keighley, West Yorkshire, BD21 4PQ
Tel: 01535 664222
www.designeryarns.uk.com

Jaeger
(USA) Westminster Fibres Inc.
4 Townsend West, Suite 8, Nashua, NH 03063
Tel: (603) 886 5041
e-mail: jaeger@westminsterfibers.com
(UK) Jaeger Handknits
Green Lane Mill, Holmfirth, HD9 2DX
Tel: 01484 680050
e-mail: mail@knitrowan.com
(AUS) Australian Country Spinners
314-320 Albert Street, Brunswick, Victoria 3056
Tel: 3 9380 3888
e-mail: sales@auspinners.com.au

Louisa Harding
www.louisaharding.co.uk
(USA) Knitting Fever Inc.
315 Bayview Avenue, Amityville, NY 11701
Tel: 001 516 5463600
e-mail: knittingfever@knittingfever.com
www.knittingfever.com

(UK) Designer Yarns Ltd
Units 8–10 Newbridge Industrial Estate, Pitt Street,
Keighley, West Yorkshire,
BD21 4PQ
Tel: 01535 664222
www.designeryarns.uk.com

Noro
(USA) Knitting Fever Inc.
315 Bayview Avenue, Amityville, NY 11701
Tel: 001 516 5463600
e-mail: knittingfever@knittingfever.com
www.knittingfever.com
(UK) Designer Yarns Ltd,
Units 8–10 Newbridge Industrial Estate, Pitt Street,
Keighley, West Yorkshire, BD21 4PQ
Tel: 01535 664222
www.designeryarns.uk.com
(AUS) Prestige Yarns Pty Ltd
PO Box 39, Bulli, NSW 2516
Tel: +61 02 4285 6669
e-mail: info@prestigeyarns.com
www.prestigeyarns.com

Patons
(USA) 320 Livingstone Avenue South, Listowel, ON
Canada N4W 3H3
Tel: 1-888-368-8401
www.patonsyarns.com
(UK) Coats Crafts UK
PO Box 22, Lingfield House, McMullen Road,
Darlington, County Durham, DL1 1YQ
Tel: 01325 394237
e-mail: consumer.ccuk@coats.com
www.coatscrafts.co.uk

Rowan
www.knitrowan.com
(USA) Rowan USA
4 Townsend West, Suite 8, Nashua, NH 03063
Tel: (603) 886 5041
e-mail: rowan@westminsterfibers.com
(UK) Rowan
Green Lane Mill, Holmfirth, HD9 2DX
Tel: 01484 681881
e-mail: mail@knitrowan.com
(AUS) Australian Country Spinners
314–320 Albert Street, Brunswick, Victoria 3056
Tel: 3 9380 3888
e-mail: sales@auspinners.com.au

Rowan Classic Yarns (RCY)
www.ryclassic.com
(USA) Westminster Fibres Inc
4 Townsend West, Suite 8, Nashua, NH 03063
Tel: (603) 886 5041
e-mail: ryc@westminsterfibers.com
(UK) RYC
Green Lane Mill, Holmfirth, HD9 2BR
Tel: 01484 681881
e-mail: mail@ryclassic.com
(AUS) Australian Country Spinners
314–320 Albert Street, Brunswick, Victoria 3056
Tel: 3 9380 3888
e-mail: sales@auspinners.com.au

Sirdar
www.sirdar.co.uk
(USA) Knitting Fever Inc
315 Bayview Avenue, Amityville, NY 11701
Tel: 001 516 5463600
e-mail: knittingfever@knittingfever.com
www.knittingfever.com
(UK) Sirdar Spinning Ltd
Flanshaw Lane, Alverthorpe, Wakefield, WF2 9ND
Tel: 01924 371501
e-mail: enquiries@sirdar.co.uk
(AUS) Creative Images
PO Box 106, Hastings, Victoria 3915
Tel: 03 5979 1555
e-mail: creative@peninsula.starway.net.au

Twilleys
www.twilleys.co.uk
(UK) Twilleys of Stamford
Roman Mill, Stamford PE9 1BG
Tel: 01780 752661
e-mail: twilleys@tbramsden.co.uk

Handbag Handles
Prym range of handles
Prym Consumer USA Inc
PO Box 5028 Spartanburg, SC 29304
www.prym-consumer-usa.com

Clover range of handles
Clover Needlecraft, Inc.
13438 Alondra Blvd.
Cerritos, CA 90703 USA
e-mail: cni@clover-usa.com
www.clover-usa.com

Other handles
(USA) M & J Trimming
1008 6th Avenue (between 37th and 38th Streets)
New York, New York 10018
Tel: 1-800-9-MJTRIM or 212-204-9595
www.mjtrim.com
(UK) Kleins
5 Noel Street, London, W1F 8GD
Tel: 020 7437 6162
e-mail: mail@kleins.co.uk
www.kleins.co.uk
(UK) MacCulloch & Wallis
25–26 Dering Street, London, W1S 1AT
Tel: 020 7629 0311
e-mail: macculloch@psilink.co.uk
(UK) Get Knitted
Unit 2B, Barton Hill Trading Estate,
Herapath Street, Barton Hill, Bristol,
BS5 9RD
Tel: 0117 941 2600
e-mail: sales@getknitted.com
www.getknitted.com

about the author

Claire Crompton has worked in the knitting industry for almost 20 years. After a Knitwear Design degree she became a pattern designer for major yarn manufacturers such as Sirdar and DMC, and is the author of *The Knitter's Bible* and *The Knitter's Bible: Knitted Accessories*. She lives in Gunnislake, Cornwall. See Claire's website for more information: www.clairecrompton.co.uk.

acknowledgments

I would like to thank Sue Morgan at Viridian (getknitted.com) for supplying the GGH yarns and DMC Creative World Ltd for the tapestry wools. Thanks also to Lorna Yabsley for the fantastic photography and to the models. At David & Charles, thanks go to Cheryl Brown, Jennifer Fox-Proverbs, Bethany Dymond and Prudence Rogers for creating this book. Finally, thanks to Nicola Hodgson for editing once again.

index